# SKILL BUILDING
# FOR BEGINNING GOLF

# SKILL BUILDING FOR BEGINNING GOLF

**M. Rhonda Folio**
*Tennessee Technological University*

**Robert W. Nichols**
*PGA Golf Professional and Owner*
*Ironwood Golf Course*
*Tennessee Technological University*

**Allyn and Bacon**
Boston • London • Toronto • Sydney • Tokyo • Singapore

*Senior Series Editor:* Suzy Spivey
*Editorial Assistant:* Amy Braddock
*Marketing Manager:* Quinn Perkson
*Production Administrator:* Susan Brown
*Editorial-Production Service:* Matrix Productions Inc.
*Cover Designer:* Suzanne Harbison
*Composition Buyer:* Linda Cox
*Manufacturing Buyer:* Suzanne Lareau

***Library of Congress Cataloging-in-Publication Data***

Folio, M. Rhonda.
    Skill building for beginning golf / by M. Rhonda Folio, Robert W.
(Bobby) Nichols.
        p.   cm.
    Includes bibliographical references (p. ) and index.
    ISBN 0-205-16006-9
    1. Golf.   I. Nichols, Robert W.   II. Title.
GV965.F565   1997
796.352—dc20                                                96-34642
                                                                CIP

Printed in the United States of America

10  9  8  7  6  5  4  3  2          01  00  99  98

# Dedication

To Charles McKay, M.D. and Sandy McKay, R.N., William McDonald, M.D., Houston Sarratt, M.D., and Michael Spalding, M.D. for helping me to overcome non-Hodgkin's lymphoma, enabling me to continue this project and play golf again.

To Gib and Carolyn Hill, Tom and Martha Willis, Brenda Brooks and Connie Nichols for being there when they were needed.

To two of the greatest golfing friends, Jim Lansford and Larry Wheeler.

To all my friends and colleagues who helped me get through a major physical illness with their thoughts and prayers, so that I could continue my profession and play golf again.

To Robert W. (Bobby) Nichols, an outstanding professional golfer, coach, teacher, and my good friend and colleague, without whom this book would not have been possible.

Rhonda

I would like to dedicate this book to the following people:

In memory of my mother and father, Jim and Cora Nichols, who made great sacrifices on behalf of my best interests; and for their knowledge, wisdom, values, and love that they gave me. To my sister Reba Stamps, who loves me as she does her own children; brothers Earl, Glen, and John, who always supported me in all of my endeavors; good friend Bobby Greenwood, who has worked tirelessly to help me with my game; close friend Billie Cameron and her family for all of their support and love; good friend Joe Otto for helping me obtain my first position as a golf professional; very good friend Rhonda Folio, who has displayed more courage in times of distress than anyone I have ever known, and for all of her hard work put forth in writing this book; many friends I have made, who have positively influenced my life.

Bobby Nichols

# CONTENTS

# PREFACE

*Skill Building for Beginning Golf* was written for those individuals who wish to take a sequential skill-building process for learning beginning golf skills and the game of golf itself. The idea for this book originated after coauthor Rhonda Folio observed Robert W. (Bobby) Nichols teaching golf classes. The skill with which he taught and his ability to communicate with effective teaching cues inspired the idea for writing a golf text for those beginning their first steps at learning the game of golf.

The content will provide opportunities for effective learning and mastering beginning golf skills. Many of the learning ideas are based on Bobby Nichols's extensive professional golf playing, coaching, and teaching activities and Rhonda Folio's teaching experiences, research, and publications about the learning of motor skills. Many of the learning strategies and drills have been used and validated in golf classes taught by both of the authors and by having individuals evaluate the activities and provide verbal feedback about their effectiveness.

The beginner will find the skill analysis approach and sequentially arranged drills an easy method for learning at a self-paced schedule. The work contains many interactive drills in which learners keep track of their progress based on goals established for most of the drills. Other features include "Skill Builder Checklists" to check skill-building progress. These serve as an abbreviated guide while practicing. They may also be used as measures in a mastery learning approach to golf skills.

The authors believe in practice, conditioning, and proper nutrition as additional skills to build for better golf. Chapters are devoted to these topics.

One of the most important skills for beginners to develop is to learn to be one's own coach. By learning basic concepts related to the golf swing, the learner will be able to monitor progress and determine a practice strategy for continued skill building. With the Round Summary Log, Goal Mastery Sheet, and Practice Strategy Log, each golfer will be able to determine strengths and weaknesses, define goals, and develop a practice strategy. Additionally, common errors and corrections are noted for each skill. This text aids new golfers in becoming their own coaches.

Although this work was written for beginning golfers, the content will also assist more advanced players. Whether the golfer uses the text as a supplement to a golf class or as a self-paced learning tool, we hope it will bring success to all who use it.

Teaching others how to teach golf seemed to be one of the most important supplements to the content. This work is accompanied by an *Instructor's Guide*, which assists those teaching beginning golf with organizational ideas, presentation concepts, teaching strategies, sample lesson plans, ideas for teacher-made equipment, key phrases to use, and modifications for teaching people with disabilities. Other elements of the guide include a test bank, overhead transparency masters, and skills tests.

# ACKNOWLEDGMENTS

The writing of this book has been a real pleasure. There are several individuals who have assisted in some way in making this project a reality and interesting. These individuals deserve a great deal of thanks and gratitude for their contributions.

The terrific individuals who modeled pictures for the figures include: Shawn Floyd, Major Warner, and Chris Lockard for rules pictures; Ramona Pennington for conditioning exercises and comments on proper technique; Lorenzo Rivers for conditioning and strength training; Scott Manzaro for putting; Greg Wyatt for pitch shots; Katrina Parker and Jay Underwood for chip shots; Melanie Gray, alignment and posture; Wade Morrell for the full swing; Chad Foster for specialty shots; and Misty McKee and Nicki Wolfe for etiquette.

Thanks to Dr. Flavious Smith, Chair of Health and Physical Education, Tennessee Tech University, for allowing Rhonda to teach beginning golf and for his encouragement to write this book. Thanks to our other colleagues in Health and Physical Education, Evans Brown, Lebron Bell, Bob and Ann Johnston, and Steve Smith, for being supportive.

Thanks to Dr. Karen Adams for being a flexible boss and allowing and encouraging faculty to pursue professional interests, which allowed the development of this work and its smooth progress.

Also, thanks to Jeff Huddleston, who developed the pictures for this book at Cookeville Camera and for many helpful suggestions; to Connie Nichols for secretarial support and generally adding humor to the work environment, for being a good beginning golf student, and for giving feedback about some of the Skill Builder Activities; to all the students who have taken beginning golf, for their teaching us as much as we have taught them. Many of the strategies were tried with our classes, and feedback was obtained.

And, finally, thanks to Suzy Spivey and Lisa Davidson, two very supportive editors of the HPER division of Allyn & Bacon, for their encouragement, editorial assistance, and patience; to Michael Griffin, Valdosta State University;

Joseph Lopour, Southern Utah University; Peggy McDonald, Central Piedmont Community College; Scott Moe, Valdosta State University; and to Marilyn Ross, University of Pittsburg, for their reviews of the book; and to Merrill Peterson of Matrix Productions for editorial assistance.

# ABOUT THE AUTHORS

## M. Rhonda Folio

M. Rhonda Folio earned her bachelor of science degree in physical education at George Peabody College of Vanderbilt University. She earned her masters at the University of South Florida in guidance and counseling and her EdS and EdD degrees in physical education from George Peabody College of Vanderbilt. Folio's graduate studies focused on physical education for people with disabilities, teaching, and research. She was a physical education teacher and coach for four years. Currently, as professor of Physical Education and Special Education at Tennessee Technological University, Cookeville, Tennessee, Folio focuses her teaching and research on motor skill development, golf teaching methods, special education, and physical education teacher training methods. Courses she teaches frequently include beginning golf, physical education, and special education. Publications include a text on adapted physical education, a nationally standardized test and curriculum on motor skill development, a video series on children's skills from birth to three, and several journal articles related to special education and physical education. Folio assists with the Tennessee Tech Men's Golf Team and is an avid amateur golfer.

### Robert W. (Bobby) Nichols

Bobby Nichols is a PGA golf professional with more than 30 years playing and teaching experience. Nichols earned his bachelor of science degree in physical education from Tennessee Technological University. Between 1970 and 1973 he played on the PGA Tour. He has won more than 90 professional golf tournaments and was chosen as Spalding's Golf Professional of the year in 1992 and Tennessee's Professional Golf Player of the Year in 1970 and 1976. Nichols also qualified and played in three PGA Championships and the United States Senior Open in 1991 and 1995. He was elected to the Tennessee Tech Sports Hall of Fame in 1991. In 1992, he won the Tennessee State Open Championship. Currently, Nichols is the owner and head PGA golf professional of Ironwood Golf Course in Cookeville, Tennessee. Serving as the Tennessee Tech men's and women's golf coach, he received the Coach of the Year Award in 1990, and his 1991 team won the Ohio Valley Conference Championship. He continues to play professionally, teach golf, and coach golf for the TTU men's and women's golf teams.

# INTRODUCTION

Congratulations! You have decided to learn how to play the wonderful game of golf. Thousands like yourself are selecting the game of golf as a major leisure-time activity. *Skill Building for Beginning Golf* is a text designed with the beginning golfer in mind. The book is structured in a way that allows the learner to read the information in understandable terms, view the pictures of each skill, and follow the "Skill Building Activities" that are analyzed to bring the golfer a step-by-step learning sequence for each skill. "Skill Builder Checklists" are designed to carry the golfer through each skill step. The authors firmly believe that the approach to learning golf in this text will provide the beginner early success and progress toward mastery of each skill.

Golf can be frustrating at times. When things seem to go wrong, review the skill checklists and activities to refresh your memory. Above all, review the fundamentals in the set-up. It takes time and dedication to achieve golf knowledge and skills. This book provides suggestions for practice that will help maintain skills even when playing time is diminished. Master the basic fundamentals first, then take them to the course. Practice the skills many times before introducing the ball to the skill. Review the picture sequences to have a good visual of each skill. And accept that it takes time to learn the fundamentals.

Try putting as a first skill after studying and practicing the set-up fundamentals. You will have a lot of success, at first, with putting. You may even want to move next to chipping and pitching, saving the full swing for last. You will then be skill-building your golf game. No matter what path is taken to learning this game, be patient and diligent; you will be surprised at how well you do toward the mastery of beginning golf. Most of all, remember why you chose to play golf—mainly for fun! Keep fun in your learning activities.

Almost all directions are given for the right-handed player. Left-handed golfers will have to reverse the directions to fit the left hand. This is really not difficult to do. Good luck with your game, and play well!

# 1

# THE GAME OF GOLF

This chapter will discuss the game of golf, including the purpose of and the overall concept of the game. Many play golf simply to enjoy themselves in beautiful settings, some are fierce competitors.

The typical structure of a golf course, illustrated and explained to familiarize the learner, accompanies a general description of how the game is played, as well as descriptions of equipment, how each piece is used in playing a round of golf and distances hit by various clubs. You will learn what makes up a starter set of clubs, the characteristics of clubs, and care of your equipment.

## Learner Skills

1. Describe the basic equipment needed to play a round of golf.
2. Explain how to care for equipment.
3. Describe how the game of golf is played.
4. Describe the characteristics and composition of a golf course.

## Prerequisite Skills

1. The desire and motivation to learn the great game of golf.

## PURPOSES FOR PLAYING GOLF

Public golf courses became prevalent in major cities in the United States by the 1920s and have continued to develop since then. Golf resorts and courses around the world range from fancy resorts to small-town courses. You won't have to travel to an exotic spot to find a good golf course; there is probably one in your hometown or within an easy drive: private membership courses, combination member and public courses, and public courses.

Golf is played in some of the most breathtaking surroundings in the world. Nearly two-thirds or more of the golf rounds in the United States are played on public courses. Many players retreat to golf resorts for vacations, but you do not have to belong to a private course to enjoy a round of golf, nor does it cost a lot to play on many public courses, especially if you walk.

Golf is a lot of fun in many ways. Recalling great shots made in a round with friends or meeting new friends while on a golfing vacation make the game most enjoyable; so does understanding enough about the game to appreciate watching a great PGA or LPGA golf professional play a top-notch round; not to mention making a hole in one! Those who love competition and a real challenge can take golf to the ultimate level of competing.

Another reason people play golf is for the exercise, particularly if they walk the course. Walking allows play to happen at a leisurely pace while providing a nice workout. Golf is a game for a lifetime. It can be played by seniors well into their 80s or more. If you learn the fundamentals of the game, you can play and enjoy it for decades.

## PURPOSE OF THE GAME

The purpose of the game of golf is to hit a ball into a small hole (cup) on a grassy area (green) in as few strokes as possible from the starting point (tee). Each attempt made to swing at the ball, whether the ball is contacted or not, counts as a stroke. The point is to make as few strokes as possible on each hole, of which there are eighteen on a regulation golf course.

## THE GOLF COURSE AND PLAYING THE GAME

The golf course is the designated playing area, which includes "through the green" and all "hazards." The length of courses varies from 5,600 yards to 7,200 yards. Of the eighteen holes on a regulation course, short-length holes are called par threes, medium-length holes are usually par fours, and long holes are par fives. "Par" is the designed score of excellence to get the ball from the tee into the hole. You are actually playing against par if you play by yourself. A golfer who shoots par for a round of golf is referred to as a "scratch golfer."

A complete game of golf is called a "round." You score the round by counting the number of strokes it takes to hit the ball from the tee into the cup for each hole. The score is recorded on a scorecard with a place to write in the number of strokes for each hole. At the end of the round, the score for each hole is totaled, and this becomes the score for the round.

## Parts of the Course

**Teeing Ground.**    The starting point from which to hit the ball is called the tee or teeing ground. It will have markers to designate the tee. Usually, there are several tees that are color coded. Blue tees are the farthest from the hole and generally are played by scratch golfers or other excellent players. White tees are several yards in front of the blue tees and are referred to as men's regular tees. This does not mean that only men may play from these tees. Women who drive the ball well and who are excellent golfers may also play from the white or blue tees. Figure 1.1 depicts a typical golf hole. Gold tees are closer to the hole than white tees and are usually designated for senior male golfers. Red tees have several yards' advantage over the white tees and are generally used by women golfers.

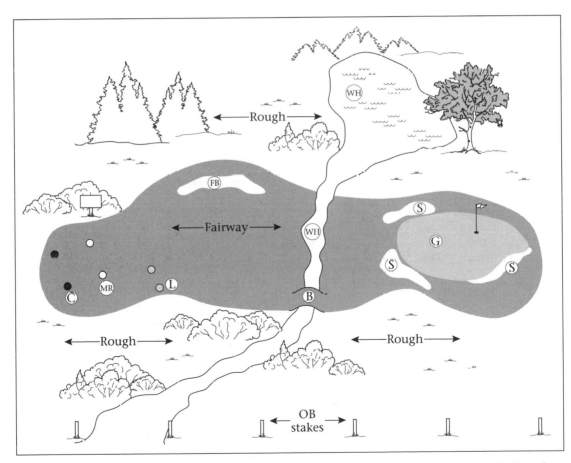

**FIGURE 1.1    Typical Golf Hole.** Legend: C = Championship Tees, MR = Men's Regular Tees (white), L = Ladies' Tees (red), FB = Fairway Bunker, G = Green, S = Sand Bunker, WH = Water Hazard, OB = Out of Bounds, B = Bridge

**Through the Green.**   The area of the course between the tee and the green is called "through the green." This portion of the hole is divided into two sections called the "fairway," or the center portion, which has grass cut fairly short. The surrounding outer edges of the fairway are referred to as the "rough," which is usually cut somewhat higher than the fairway. It is more difficult to hit a ball from the rough because of the height of the grass. The best place to play the ball is from the fairway where the short grass grows.

**The Green.**   The putting surface where the hole or cup is located is called the green. Here the grass is cut very close so the ball will roll smoothly when it is putted. The green is at the opposite end of the tee. On very long holes you may not see the green until you are ready to hit your second shot. The hole is on the green and is moved regularly, to different locations on the green, to keep the green from wearing in one spot.

**Hazards.**   Hazards are also located along the hole. Two types of hazards exist. "Bunkers" are depressions filled with sand alongside the fairway and green. Some are natural and filled with grass. Most, however, are constructed and strategically placed by the golf course architect.

"Water hazards" include streams, lakes, rivers, and seas. If your ball should have the unfortunate experience of resting in the hazard, special rules apply when playing the ball. A direct water hazard, which may be a river, lake, or stream, is referred to in the USGA Rule Book as a "water hazard" if it runs across the fairway. It is marked by yellow stakes. A "lateral water hazard" is water that runs parallel to the fairway; it is marked by red stakes.

**Out of Bounds.**   Out-of-bounds areas on the course are marked by white stakes or fences. These are usually designated on the scorecard. Holes may have out-of-bounds areas on both sides of the rough, on one side of the rough, or behind the green. Some holes have no out of bounds.

**Types of Holes/Par.**   Par, being the designated standard for each hole, includes the number of strokes it should take to get the ball from the tee into the hole. Par three means that you are allowed one tee shot to reach the green and two putts. A par four allows one tee shot, an approach shot from the fairway or rough to reach the green, and two putts. A par five allows one tee shot, two approach shots to reach the green, and two putts.

The length of par three holes may range from 90 to 230 yards; par fours are 245 to 445 yards; par fives are the longest holes, ranging from 445 to 585 yards. Typically, on a regulation golf course, there are four par threes, ten par fours, and four par fives making up the eighteen holes. Par for a golf course is usually 72, sometimes 71. Men and women usually have the same par on most courses.

## Names of Scores

Certain scores on some holes have names. A ball that rolls into the hole on a par 3 from the tee shot is called a "hole in one" or "ace." A score of 1 less than par on a hole is called a "birdie." Therefore, a score of 2 on a par 3 is called a birdie, as is a score of 3 on a par 4 and a score of 4 on a par 5. An "eagle" is a score of 2 below par on a given hole. Thus, a score of 3 on a par 5 is called an eagle. A score of 1 over par for a hole is called a "bogey." So a score of 4 on a par 3 is called a bogey. It is not unusual for players to score 2 over par on a hole, particularly when incurring a penalty. Two over par is called a "double bogey." Of course one can go even higher on a hole: Three over par, for example, is called a "triple bogey." If a player gets a score of 4 over par on a hole, it is called a "quadruple bogey." Most golfers try their best to avoid such scores, but as golf goes, it is not always possible, even among the best of players. Beginning golfers should not be so concerned about their scores while they learn to play. Just play to have fun and enjoy the game.

## Scorecard

Keeping your score for a round of golf is easy. The scorecard (Figure 1.2) provides good information about the course. Most cards contain the following: the yardage for each hole from each tee; par for each hole; the handicap or difficulty of each hole; the total yardage for the front and back nine; and the total par for each nine. The front nine is called "Out" and the back nine is called "In." There is a line on which to write the player's name and handicap index if one has been established. The handicap on each hole lets you know where you would get a stroke or strokes subtracted from your total score. The strokes you subtract from your total score, based on your handicap, will give the net score. Also, if playing an official match, two players should sign the scorecard to attest that it is correct.

## Game Components

Golf is often said to have several components. There are four main components to the game—the short game, long game, course management, or strategy and mental aspects of play.

**Short Game.** The short game is made up of putting, chipping, and pitching. These are played with the short clubs, such as the pitching wedge, 9-iron, and 8-iron, although chipping may be done with 6- and 5-irons. The short game is made up of the strokes used most often during a round of play. The putting stroke is the one most frequently used in a round of golf. Therefore, it is

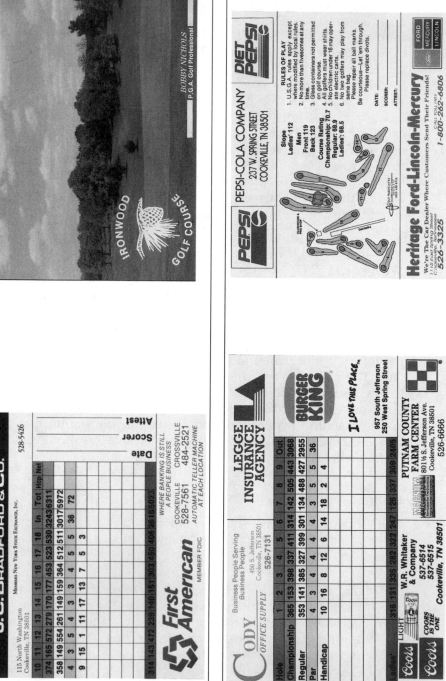

important to practice this shot and all others in the short game because this is where a golfer can save many strokes. Remember, two putts are allowed in a score of par. You can really drive up your score by having two or three extra putts on a hole.

**Long Game.**   The long game is made up of tee shots, or drives, fairway wood shots, and long approach shots with the long irons such as the 5-, 4- and 3-irons.

**Course Management.**   A third component of the game is how a player manages the course. A golf hole has strengths and weaknesses. Its strengths may be a tight pin placement on the green or several greenside bunkers. A weakness may be a large landing area for tee shots. Course management consists of deciding how to play each shot on a hole, which club to select under given situations, plotting shots from tee to green, avoiding landing in hazards, and finding a good target at which to aim. It also consists of knowing your strengths and weaknesses with golf skills and matching them to the hole.

**Mental Aspects.**   A fourth part of the game is the mental aspects. Most beginners concentrate on the physical aspects of golf and devote little time to the mental. The mental side of golf is the way in which you prepare your mind to execute each shot. Mental aspects of the game include tension control, focusing and maintaining your attention on each shot, visualizing each shot, and having self-confidence to execute it. It also involves how you react and cope with other situations around you on the course.

## Rules

The rules of the game must also be learned if a person is to be a knowledgeable golfer. Rules assist players in competing fairly, whether against the course or one another. When the rules are violated, certain penalties can be incurred. Chapter 8 is devoted to covering the basic rules and procedures for play.

## Etiquette

Golf is considered a very polite game; it is supposed to be a game of honesty. When you play, you must be considerate and play by the rules. Your conduct as you play the game of golf is often referred to as "etiquette." Whether a person plays in a group or as an individual, it is etiquette that governs order of play, behavior on the entire course, procedures on the green, regard for other players, playing without delay, and taking care of the golf course.

**Dressing for Play.**   Dress is important on the course. This does not mean that you have to wear designer golf shirts, but it does mean that appropriate attire be worn. Golf courses generally have their own requirements on acceptable attire for play. Check these before you decide to play at a particular course.

## EQUIPMENT

Today, there are all types of golf equipment on the market. It can be confusing as to what a beginner should purchase, and the cost varies greatly. One sure thing to do about purchasing equipment is to see a professional who can fit you properly with the clubs that are best suited to your needs and body composition.

Clubs consist of irons and woods. Traditionally, woods were made of hardwood, such as persimmon. Today, woods are also made of metal or graphite. Woods are numbered typically 1 through 9. The 1-wood is referred to as the driver. The 3-wood and driver are used mostly for long tee shots; 5- and 7- or 9-woods are used from the fairway to carry you to the green or leave a short shot to reach it.

Irons are numbered 1 through 9, pitching wedge, and sand wedge. Long irons, such as the 2-, 3-, and 4-irons, require a good golf swing. They hit the ball long, but there is little room for error as they do not produce much backspin on the ball. While just learning and with a high handicap, a 5-iron, 5- or 7-wood should be used instead. Mid-irons, such as the 5, 6, and 7, provide approach shots that require more distance than the short irons, such as the 8- or 9-iron and pitching wedge. Irons may also be used from the teeing ground. The short irons have the highest numbers and send the ball high with short distances. These should be used when within 100 to 130 yards of the green.

The clubs, whether they are irons or woods, have the same basic parts. Learn these parts (Figure 1.3), as well as the directions and corrections on how to hold the club, change your stance or grip, and solve problems with incorrect hits, and you'll be a player.

### Putters

Putters today come in all shapes, lengths, and materials. The head of the putter comes in different styles. Figure 1.4 illustrates various putters. It is important to choose one that fits your size and stance. Experiment with different putters and select one in which you feel confident that you will make the putt. Most golf shops have small putting surfaces, indoors, which allow you to try out different putters.

### Starter Set of Clubs

A beginning golfer does not need a full set of clubs to start play. In fact, you can get by with half a set, or seven clubs, rather than the fourteen allowed by the USGA rules. The set includes a 3- or 5-wood, 3-, 5-, 7-, 9-irons, a sand or pitching wedge, and a putter. A full set of clubs includes, typically, a driver or 3-wood, a 5-wood, 3-, 4-, 5-, 6-, 7-, 8-, 9-irons, pitching wedge, sand wedge, and putter. The golfer can configure the full set in any way suitable as long as there are no more than fourteen clubs in the bag.

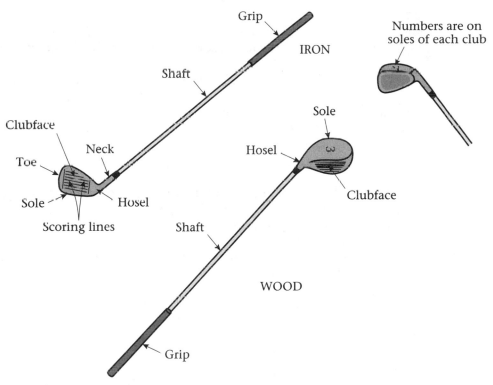

FIGURE 1.3 Club Parts

**Considerations Before Buying Clubs.** Clubs have several characteristics that need to be fitted to the individual using them. These characteristics include the length of the club, lie of the club, flex of the shaft, swing weight of the club, loft of the clubhead, and grip thickness.

*Club Lengths.* There are two standard lengths for clubs, although clubs may be designed to whatever length is needed. The length of a club should be based on your height, the length of your arms, and your posture when hitting the

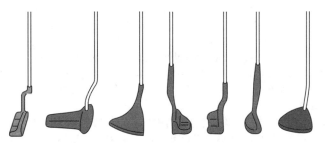

FIGURE 1.4 Various Putter Designs

ball. Men's clubs are a little longer than women's clubs. However, gender should not necessarily be the only consideration in club length. A tall female may need a man's length club. A short male may need a woman's length club.

*Lie of the Club.*    The lie of the club refers to the angle of the leading edge of the clubhead in relation to the shaft of the club. Ideally, after proper set-up to the ball, the lie of the leading edge of the clubhead should be parallel to the ground. A tall player needs a club with a more upright lie; a shorter player needs a flatter lie. Using a club with the incorrect lie results in poor shots, depending on how the golfer compensates in the swing.

*Shafts.*    Today, shafts are made of a variety of materials, the most common being steel. Graphite shafts are becoming popular, as well as other metal alloys, including titanium. These are costly, however. One important characteristic of the shaft is its flexibility. This is the amount of bend or give in the shaft. Your swing speed should determine the type of shaft you need in your clubs. Stronger players with fast swing speeds prefer stiff or regular flex shafts. The flex of a shaft ranges from stiff to flexible. Women's clubs are more flexible and are denoted with an "L-flex." An "R-flex," or regular flex, will fit the needs of most players. Again, gender should not be the major criterion for selecting a shaft for a club.

*Swing Weight.*    The swing weight consists of the club's distribution of weight from the grip to the head. Actually, clubs have a balanced weight so that clubs feel similar when they are swung. To help with a consistent swing, the longer clubs are actually lighter than the shorter clubs. Swing weights are classified by letters and range from A to E, with A being the lighter and E the heavier. A club that is too heavy will be difficult to control and manage, thus shot accuracy and distance will be affected. C swing weights are usually recommended for females; D weights are used by most males.

*Loft.*    Loft refers to the angle of the clubface or the tilt of the clubface. Each club has a standard loft that affects the trajectory of the ball flight and the amount of backspin produced on the ball. The steeper the loft, the higher the ball will fly with greater backspin. This means that it will stop rolling quicker when it lands. The higher the number on the club, the more loft it has. A 9-iron produces a higher shot than a 3-iron. So lower-lofted clubs produce more distance.

Golfers need to understand how far they hit each club so they can manage their game and the course. Figure 1.5 shows how the loft increases from the driver through the 5-wood. Note that the straighter the angle of the clubface, the less loft it has. The driver has the least amount of loft of any club in the bag except for the putter.

Consequently, little if any backspin is produced with lesser-lofted clubs. As a result, with little backspin to counteract sidespin, longer clubs require less room for error for accurate hits. Even the slightest open or closed clubface with the driver can send the ball 20 to 30 yards off center, because sidespin is not

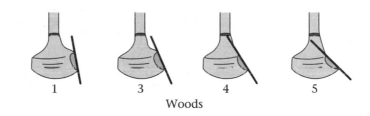

Woods

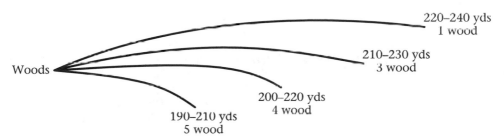

Woods

220–240 yds
1 wood

210–230 yds
3 wood

200–220 yds
4 wood

190–210 yds
5 wood

**FIGURE 1.5    Woods**

being counteracted by backspin. Sometimes golfers think that the longer clubs are harder to master than the shorter clubs. There is less room for error in terms of open or closed club faces with longer clubs. Figure 1.6 depicts the different lengths and lofts of various clubs.

The distance you hit each club is important to know. While on the practice range, and as you become more consistent, note how far, on the average, you hit each club. Write the distance down in a log and remember each one. You may hit a 7-iron, if you are a male, 120 to 140 yards. But on the average of five hits, it may be 130 yards. Women, on the average, range from 20 to 40

| Woods | Lengths – Inches | Loft – Degrees |
|---|---|---|
| Driver | 43 | 0.5–11 |
| 3 wood | 42 | 20 |
| 5 wood | 41 | 28 |

| Irons | Length – Inches | Loft – Degrees |
|---|---|---|
| 3 | 38 | 22 |
| 4 | 37½ | 26 |
| 5 | 37 | 30 |
| 6 | 36½ | 34 |
| 7 | 36 | 38 |
| 8 | 35½ | 42 |
| 9 | 35 | 46 |
| Pitching Wedge | 35 | 52 |
| Sand Wedge | 35 | 58 |

**FIGURE 1.6    Standard Club Lengths and Lofts**

| Club | Distance (Men) Yards | Distance (Women) Yards |
|---|---|---|
| Driver | 200 + | 170 + |
| 3-wood | 180 + | 150 + |
| 5-wood | 150–180 | 140–170 |
| 3-iron | 160–185 | 140–165 |
| 4-iron | 140–175 | 130–150 |
| 5-iron | 140–165 | 120–135 |
| 6-iron | 130–150 | 110–125 |
| 7-iron | 120–140 | 100–115 |
| 8-iron | 110–130 | 90–105 |
| 9-iron | 90–120 | 70–95 |

**FIGURE 1.7   Distance Differences Between Men and Women**

yards less per club than males. Figure 1.7 provides, as a general rule, the difference in distances between males and females for each club.

*Grip.*   The grip of the club is the portion of the shaft which players hold. The material is usually leather or rubber. Selecting the proper grip width is extremely important.

A grip that is too small or thin will increase the action of the hands and probably produce more hook shots. A grip that is too large will most likely contribute to sliced shots. In a grip that is too thin or small, the fingers touch and overlap the palm of the hand. In a grip that is too large, space appears between the fingers and the palm. In a properly fitting grip, the middle finger contacts the palm (Figure 1.8).

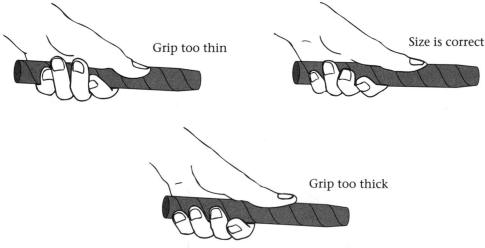

Grip too thin

Size is correct

Grip too thick

**FIGURE 1.8   Grip Size**

## Golf Balls

There are many manufacturers of golf balls. They all have a size of 1.68 inches in diameter and weigh 1.62 ounces.

**Two-Piece Ball.**  This ball has a solid center made of synthetic material. A cover is then placed over the hard center. This is a popular and durable type of ball. These balls come in different colors—white, yellow, and orange. Beginners would probably do best to use a two-piece, surlyn-covered ball, as they are resistant to cuts.

**Compression.**  The relative hardness of a golf ball refers to compression. Today the compression on most golf balls is indicated by the numbers 80, 90, and 100. As it is hit with the clubface, a ball with a compression of number 100 feels harder than one of 80 and travels farther.

## Tees

Tees are used to hit the ball from the teeing ground. Tees are made of wood, plastic, and now of biodegradable material. The only place you are officially allowed to hit the ball from a tee is on the teeing ground.

## Glove

A golf glove is generally worn on the left hand for right-handed golfers. This helps to provide a solid-feeling grip. The glove will also help to absorb sweat, keeping your hand from slipping on the club. Gloves are made from leather or other materials.

## Shoes

Golf shoes come with spikes or without. Spikes offer good footing during the swing. If you walk a lot when you play golf, invest in a good quality golf shoe. Athletic shoes without cleats are also appropriate for play.

## Golf Bag

There are as many golf bags as there are balls and shoes. Some bags are heavy, being made of leather or vinyl. Beginners with a starter set of clubs do not need a large bag. A smaller one will do. A good strap is important to consider, especially if you walk and carry your bag. It is also a good idea to get a lightweight bag if you plan to carry it.

## Equipment Care

Your investment in good equipment will last longer if what you buy is maintained and protected. Keep your equipment as dry as possible. Most bags come with head covers to keep your clubs dry.

**Clubs.**   Keep clubs clean and dry. Woods made of wood should not be stored in damp places. Do not let mud get caked in the grooves of the clubs. A club brush can be purchased to scrub out dirt during play. Be careful how you place the clubs in your bag. Do not shove them in the bag so tightly that the grips become torn.

Wash clubs in warm soapy water and dry them. The grips should be washed and dried—this will help to keep them tacky. When they become smooth and worn, replace them. Proshops or golf specialty stores hire personnel qualified to change grips.

---

**Skill Builders**

GOLF COURSE STRUCTURE

*Purpose:* Become familiar with the structure of a typical golf hole.

*Equipment:* illustration of a golf hole without parts of the hole labeled.

*Activity:* The group leader has the overhead or labeled sheet. Ask someone to name a part of the hole, such as the teeing ground. Students should label the part named. Continue until all parts are named and marked on the sheets.

CLUB PARTS

Repeat the same activity with golf course structure.

BEGINNER SET OF CLUBS

*Purpose:* Name the clubs that make up a starter set.

*Equipment:* list of clubs that make a starter set

*Activity:* The leader of the group asks for the names of the clubs in a starter set. As a club is identified, it is selected from a group of clubs. Continue until all clubs are correctly identified and selected.

INDIVIDUAL SKILL BUILDERS

1. Determine what the rules of golf cover.
2. What are the game components of golf?
3. Define par.
4. What are the names of certain scores, i. e., bogey, birdie?
5. What does etiquette cover in golf?
6. Describe how to take care of golf equipment.

# 2

# THE SET-UP: PREPARING TO SWING

A major portion of the golf swing is based on preparation to make the swing. How you hold the club, stand, position and align your body create the foundation for making a correct swing. These fundamentals are referred to as the "set-up," or "address," which includes the grip, stance and posture, ball position, and alignment. Each of these fundamentals must be present and correct to produce a mechanically sound swing. The golfer should understand how each of these fundamentals affects the swing and flight of the ball. A significant amount of time must be spent on developing these fundamentals. This means practicing the set-up elements correctly until they become routine. Emphasizing the correct set-up in the beginning will eliminate many swing errors.

## Learner Skills

1. Explain the fundamentals necessary for preparing to make a golf swing.
2. Demonstrate the correct set-up for executing the golf swing.

## Prerequisite Skills

1. Knows the parts of the club.
2. Has a concept of the game of golf.

## SET-UP: PREPARING TO SWING

### Grip

Author Chuck Hogan (1993) prefers to call the grip the "hold." Why? You actually hold the club. Gripping it may lead golfers to believe that you squeeze the club. The grip, or how you hold the club, is essential to a proper swing. Holding the club improperly starts the golfer off at the beginning on the wrong track. All of the clubs are held the same except for the putter.

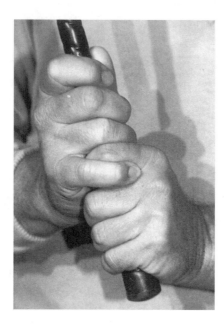

**FIGURE 2.1   Overlapping Vardon Grip.** Right little finger overlaps left index finger.

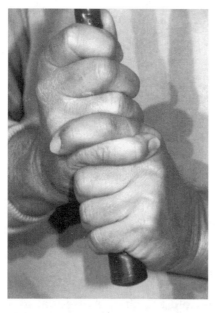

**FIGURE 2.2   Interlocking Grip.** Little finger of the right hand interlocks with left index finger.

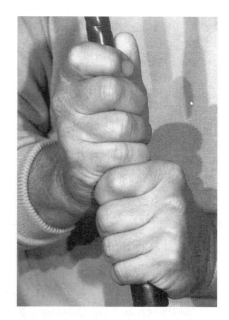

**FIGURE 2.3   Ten-Finger Grip.** Recommended for use if hands are small.

A key to a good grip, or hold, on the club is that the hands must be placed on the grip of the club so they work together and do not fight each other. The hands must work as a unit, with the palms facing each other. The placement of your hands and grip pressure can impact the direction the ball will travel and the tempo of the swing.

**Grip Types.**   There are basically three ways to hold the club to execute the swing. These are referred to as the Overlapping/Vardon, interlocking, and ten-finger grips. Figures 2.1, 2.2, and 2.3 illustrate each type of grip.

People with small hands might be more successful in using the ten-finger grip. Some professionals do not recommend the interlocking grip, as it places the club more in the palm of the right hand.

**Steps for Gripping the Club.**

*Left Hand.*   The left hand grips the club first (Figure 2.4A). Before you grip the club, be sure that the leading edge of the clubface is aligned with the hand of a clock at the 12 o'clock position in front of you on the ground.

With your right hand, hold the club steadily and place the grip diagonally across the left palm so the club contacts the second joint of the index finger and rests under the heel pad of the palm (Figure 2.4B). Then gently close your left hand around the club. The hand is positioned somewhat like it would be when gripping a pistol (Figure 2.5).

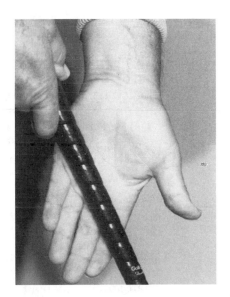

**FIGURE 2.4A   Left Hand on Grip.** Note the thumb is even with the first finger. A "V" is formed by the left thumb and index finger.

**FIGURE 2.4B   Side View Left Hand.** Note the handle against the heel of the left palm. The club rests next to the base of the fingers and against the heel of the palm.

**FIGURE 2.5   Club Position in Relation
to the Palm.** The butt end of the club
should be braced against the heel of the
palm. The club is held in the fingers.

The heel pad of your left hand should be about one-half inch below the butt
end of the club, with a small portion of the club extending beyond the heel of
the left hand. The heel of the palm should be slightly on top of the club and
not under it (Figure 2.5).

Hold the club in front of you, raised a little above parallel. In Figure 2.4A,
when you look at your left hand, a "V" is formed by the thumb and index finger. The "V" should point at a spot between your right ear and right shoulder.
The left thumb should be about even with the first knuckle of the index finger, with little or no gap between them. The left thumb should rest on the grip
just right of center. You should see two knuckles when you look at your hand.

*Right Hand.*   The right hand holds the club more in the fingers than in the
palm. The middle fingers, at the middle joint, go under the club (Figures 2.6A
and B). Rest the index finger on the shaft and the thumb on the center of the
shaft and lightly hold the club.

The thumb of the left hand should now fit against the thumb side pad of
the right hand (Figure 2.7). The hands should be close together. The "V"
formed by the thumb and index finger of the right hand should be parallel to
the "V" of the left hand.

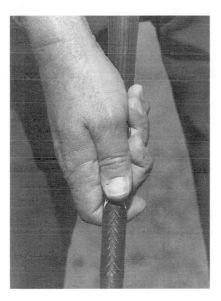

**FIGURE 2.6A Right Hand on Grip.** A "V" is formed by the thumb and index or first finger.

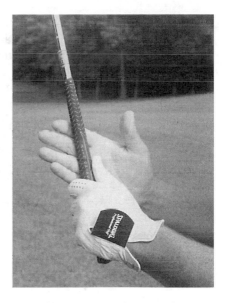

**FIGURE 2.6B Right Hand on Grip.** The right hand holds the club mostly in the last three fingers, between the second and third joints.

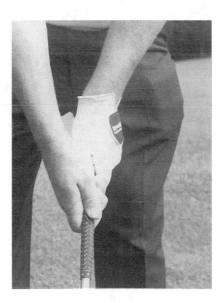

**FIGURE 2.7 Both Hands on Grip.** "Vs" point between ear and mid-right shoulder.

The little finger of the right hand should rest over the forefinger of the left hand, producing the overlapping grip; or for the interlocking grip, it should interlock with the index finger of the left hand; or for the ten-finger grip, it should be next to the left index finger. The thumb and forefinger of the right hand should touch each other lightly. Study the pictures of the grip procedure carefully until you can picture the grip with your eyes closed. Also, the right shoulder is lower in this grip position, as the right hand is below the left, forming a triangle with the shoulders and extended arms (Figure 2.8).

The club should feel as if it is more in the fingers than in the palms. A good check is to open both hands and see if the palms face each other. This is important to be able to return the clubface square to the ball at impact. If the right hand rests too far under the grip, the palms will not be facing each other. This produces a strong right hand on the club, which usually will produce a closed clubface at impact, resulting in sidespin, producing a shot that curves left called a hook.

**FIGURE 2.8   Right Shoulder is Lower than the Left.** Toe of the club points to 12 o'clock when taking the grip. Shoulders and extended arms form a triangle.

Grips are described as neutral, strong, and weak. Figures 2.9A and B illustrate a strong and a weak grip. In some cases, it may be desirable to intentionally slice or hook the ball to hit around an obstacle. Changing the grip is one way to accomplish this. A strong grip may produce a hook, a shot that curves to the left. A weak grip may produce a slice, a shot that curves to the right.

**Grip Pressure.**    Remember to hold the club lightly. Holding the club tightly will destroy good hand work throughout the swing. Grip the club and lift it so the club points to the sky just above your waist. Hold it only tightly enough to keep it from slipping from your hands. Figure 2.10 includes a Grip Skill-Builder Checklist. Grip the club using the checklist's key points.

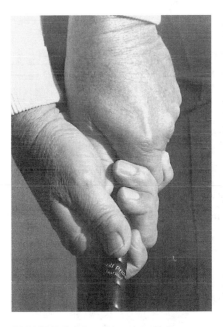

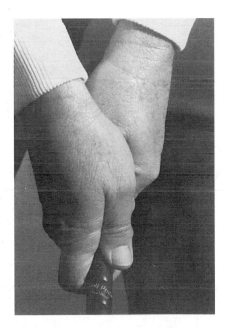

**FIGURE 2.9A    Strong Grip.**
This often produces a ball flight that curves to the left—a hook or draw. "Vs" point to the edge or outside of the right shoulder.

**FIGURE 2.9B    Weak Grip.** "Vs" point to the left of the chin. This often produces a ball flight curving to the right—a slice.

**Arms**

_____ relaxed

_____ hanging naturally

**Left Hand (Target Hand)**

_____ back of hand faces target

_____ club placed diagonally across the palm and fingers

_____ two knuckles visible

_____ "V" pointing between right ear and shoulder

**Right Hand (Rear Hand)**

_____ palm faces target

_____ club held with two middle fingers with index finger "triggered"

_____ little finger overlaps index finger of left hand (Vardon) or

_____ little finger interlocks with index finger of left hand (interlocking) or

_____ little finger is next to index finger of left hand (ten-finger)

_____ "Vs" are parallel

_____ left thumb is barely visible

**Grip Pressure**

_____ knuckles normal color instead of white

_____ club may be pulled easily from hands

**Comments:**

**FIGURE 2.10   Grip Skill Builder Checklist.**

**Grip Skill Builders**

MIRROR DRILL

_Purpose:_ Visually see and learn a correct grip.

_Equipment:_ mirror or large windows in which reflections can be seen, a 7- or 8-iron

_Activity:_ Stand in front of a mirror or window where you can see your reflection. Practice taking the grip using the procedures described in this chapter. Check for proper position of each hand in the mirror. Also, have a partner check your grip using the Skill Builder Checklist (Figure 2.10). Repeat the procedure five times. Then try it five more times without using the mirror. Have a partner repeat the procedure as you check the grip.

FEEL DRILL

_Purpose:_ Learn how the hands "feel" in the proper grip.

_Equipment:_ any club except the putter

_Activity:_

1. Partners face each other. One partner reviews grip points using the skill check list. The other partner takes the grip, then has it checked. The person taking the grip should lift the club parallel to the ground, waist high, and check the grip.

2. Note how the hands look and feel after any corrections have been made. Repeat the procedure ten times. The other partner should then repeat the same sequence.
3. Repeat this drill, taking the grip with your eyes closed. Then check with your partner or look at a mirror for accuracy. Hold the club vertically with just enough tension to keep it from slipping.

## Stance and Posture

**Stance.** Another basic principle to building a sound golf swing is assuming the correct stance and posture in the set-up to make the swing. The stance refers to how the feet are placed and the body's weight distributed. A comfortable athletic stance is used to execute the golf swing. The stance for the full swing is about shoulder width or wide enough to allow a full swing to occur without swaying or losing balance (Figure 2.11). A stance that is too narrow will not support a balanced swing, and it will promote swaying to the side. A stance that is too wide restricts a good body turn away from the ball and minimizes a good weight transfer.

**FIGURE 2.11   Stance Width for Woods and Long Irons.** Wider stance is needed with woods and long irons.

The body's weight should be about evenly distributed between both feet and on the balls of the feet. You should not sit back on the heels or forward on the toes. You should feel lively and able to transfer your weight right or left, just as if you were dancing. Some golfers like to turn the left foot a little toward the target. This stance will create balance and readiness.

**Posture.**    The correct posture is important because it affects the way the club is moved along the swing path. Figure 2.12 depicts the correct posture for building a good swing. Your upper body is flexed from the hips with your knees bent slightly. If you cannot see most of the top of your shoes, your knees are bent too much. Your back should be fairly straight. The buttocks should be extended outward, not tucked in under the hips. This will allow a free, swinging movement around your body.

**FIGURE 2.12   Posture—Set-Up.**
Note that the upper back is
straight. Hips are flexed and
buttocks extended. Knees are
flexed over midstep of feet,
which are about shoulder width
apart. Arms hang naturally from
the shoulders, remaining connected to the chest.

Your chin should be off your chest. Have you ever heard another golfer say, "Keep your head down"? By keeping your head down and tucked to your chest, you will restrict a good body coil during the swing. Your arms should hang in a relaxed, straight position, just below the shoulders. The hands generally hang just in front of your toes if your posture is correct.

It is extremely important to keep your posture consistent throughout the swing once it is correctly set. Raising up out of the posture because of poor swing mechanics destroys the efficiency of the swing movement and creates poor contact, if any at all, with the ball.

## Ball Position

In most instances for short- and mid-irons, the ball is positioned close to the center of the stance or at the lowest point of the swing arc (Figure 2.13). For woods and long irons, the ball should be positioned just forward of center (Figure 2.14) and just inside the left heel for the driver (Figure 2.15).

**FIGURE 2.13  Ball Position for Short and Mid-Irons.** Note position of club in relation to stance line and target line.

**FIGURE 2.14  Ball Position for Long Irons.** Ball is positioned just forward of center.

**FIGURE 2.15    Ball Position for Driver.** Ball is positioned inside left heel.

**Distance from the Ball.**    The distance you stand from the ball at address or set-up is also important. This affects the arc of the swing. Stand far enough away so that when you hold the club and ground it (sole it) behind the ball, your upper arms feel connected to your chest and the knuckles of your left hand fall over, or just outside, your toe line. When your arms are touching your chest, the connection to the big muscles of the body is maintained. This sets up power and force to create distance. Try to envision a discus thrower whose arms are held close to the chest or connected. This helps the thrower to throw with the entire body not just the arms. The same is true with the golf swing.

The distance that you stand from the ball changes only when you change the length of the clubs. Your body will be closer to the ball when you hit a 9-iron and farther away when you hit a 3-iron or a driver.

## Alignment

Alignment is simply placing your body in line with the clubface or in the direction in which you intend the ball to go. It is amazing how many novice and high-handicap golfers take this step so lightly, yet it is so critical. If you were going to shoot a rifle and hit a target, think about how carefully you would aim. Golf is a target game. There is nothing more frustrating than hitting a good shot and having the ball land way left or right of the target because of poor alignment. In fact, the path of the clubhead during the swing will most likely follow the same line on which you have your body aligned. The path of the clubhead dramatically affects the initial direction of the ball's flight. So you must be sure your hips, shoulders, knees, and feet are aligned properly.

**Alignment Procedure.**   Aiming the clubface and aligning your body are both part of the routine of setting up to the ball. This should be done before hitting any golf shot. Failure to do so will contribute to inaccurate results.

An easy way to understand the alignment process is to use a pair of railroad tracks as an illustration. Imagine yourself standing on one side of the tracks. The track farthest from you represents the target line or the intended line of flight of the ball (where you want the ball to go). The rail nearest you represents the stance line, or an imaginary line passing across the tip of your toes, thighs, hips and shoulders, and running parallel to the target line (Figure 2.16). Thus, the target line and stance line need to be parallel, like the railroad tracks, to create a square stance. In addition, your hips, thighs, and shoulders must also be parallel to the target line.

**FIGURE 2.16   Alignment.**
Note position of target line
and stance line. They are
parallel like railroad tracks.

If the distance between your stance and target lines is wider at the target end, instead of parallel, an open stance will be produced. Provided that the clubface is square at impact, this will produce a ball flight that goes straight to the left (a pulled shot). (See Figure 2.17.)

A closed stance results when the stance line and target line are narrower at the target end instead of parallel (Figure 2.18). This will cause the ball to travel straight to the right (a pushed shot), provided the clubface is square at impact.

**Steps in Aiming and Aligning.**

1. Find the target line by standing behind the ball so that it is between you and the target. The target may be a spot in the fairway, green, or the flagstick itself.
2. Find something on the ground no more than two feet in front of the ball that is in line with the ball and the target. Use a blade of grass, a twig, a leaf, a divot, etc. Imagine a line running between the object, the ball, and the

**FIGURE 2.17  Open Stance.** Shoulders, hips, and feet are open. The open stance line is wider at the target end.

**FIGURE 2.18  Closed Stance.** This stance promotes a push and hook shot. Shoulders are closed to the target line, and the alignment is to the right of the target. Feet are closed and the stance line is closed.

target. This is the line on which to aim the clubface. Then align your feet, hips, and shoulders.

The object, or spot on the ground, in line with the target is referred to as an intermediate target. You need this, not a spot 100 yards away, for a point of reference.

3. Keep the spot in view and walk around to the side and set the leading edge of the clubface so that it is perpendicular or square to the target line. Then align your feet so that a line across your toes would be parallel to the target line. Always square the clubface to the target line, then align your toes, hips, and shoulders parallel to the line. Remember, aim the clubface, then align your body.

Go through the same procedure each time for setting up to prepare to make a golf shot. These steps will become part of a "pre-shot routine" that you will use on every golf shot. A Set-Up Skill Builder Checklist is included in Figure 2.19. Try to set up or address the ball using the key points in the checklist.

**Grip**
____ club runs diagonally across left palm
____ "Vs" formed by thumbs and index fingers are parallel and point to area between ear lobes to middle of right shoulder
____ palms face each other
____ right hand holds club more in the base of the fingers

**Stance**
____ square foot alignment
____ weight evenly distributed over the balls of the feet
____ heels of feet about shoulder width for long clubs and slightly narrower for shorter clubs

**Posture**
____ knees slightly bent, no farther forward than the instep of the feet
____ hips flexed
____ back straight
____ arms fall naturally just over toe line
____ hips and shoulders parallel to target line

**Ball Position**
____ middle of stance on short and mid-irons
____ toward the target side of center of stance for long irons and woods
____ inside left heel for driver

**FIGURE 2.19  Set-Up Skill Builder Checklist.**

### Set-Up Skill Builders

ATHLETIC STANCE DRILL/WEIGHT SHIFT

*Purpose:* Get a feel for and demonstrate the athletic stance or posture.

*Equipment:* two golf tees, yardstick, or golf club

*Activity:*

1. Have a partner measure the width of the other's shoulders. Mark the width on the club or yardstick, then with two golf tees, mark that same width on the ground. The partner who was measured should stand with the inside of each foot next to the tees. Repeat with the other person measuring.
2. Pretend you are making a sidearm throw, moving your weight back on the right side on the backswing and returning to the left on the forwardswing and release of the imaginary ball. Repeat the imaginary throw ten times.
3. Pretend you are throwing a beach ball with both hands. Shift your weight backward to the right foot as you take the ball back and shift your weight forward onto your left foot as you toss the ball forward.
4. Pretend that you are batting a ball. As you take the bat back, shift your weight onto your right foot. As you swing forward, shift your weight to your left foot.

DISTANCE FROM THE BALL DRILL

*Purpose:* Determine correct distance to stand from the ball.

*Equipment:* 9-iron, 5-iron, and 3-wood

*Activity:* One partner sets up to a ball, then releases the 9-iron. If the hands fall toward the body, the distance is too far from the ball. If the hands fall forward, the distance is too close to the ball. If the hands hang naturally, the distance is correct. Your partner repeats the procedure with the 9-iron while the other partner observes. Each repeats the procedure with each club.

POSTURE DRILL

*Purpose:* To develop the correct posture for the set-up and full swing.

*Equipment:* mirror and 7-, 8-, or 9-iron

*Activity:*

1. Take the set-up or address position with your side toward the mirror. Check the following to see that:
   - knees are slightly flexed;
   - weight is toward the balls of your feet, not on your toes;
   - back is straight, body is flexed at the hips, buttocks are sticking out;
   - chin is up off your chest;
   - arms hang relaxed with hands falling over, or just outside of, your toe line or in a fairly straight line from your shoulders.
2. Repeat the drill with a partner and no mirror. Have your partner check the key points for posture. Repeat the drill facing the mirror.

ALIGNMENT DRILL

*Purpose:* Develop a routine for correctly aiming and aligning the clubface and body parallel to a selected target.

*Equipment:* two extra clubs or yardsticks, ball

*Activity:*

1. Place a ball on the ground. Select a target from behind the ball. Locate an intermediate target about 1 to 2 feet in front of the ball in line with the target. Assume the set-up position, aiming the clubface perpendicular or square to the target line. Then align the feet, hips, and shoulders parallel to the target line.
2. Have your partner check to see if your body is parallel to the target line by placing a club or yardstick on the target line and a club or yardstick on the ground next to your toe line. The two clubs or sticks should be parallel to each other.
3. Check the clubface position by placing a yardstick parallel to the line of the leading edge of the clubface. It should form a 90-degree angle to the target line when it is square. If you are having difficulty lining up parallel, place on the ground a yardstick that represents the target line. Then line up with the stick as a guide.

COMMON SET-UP ERRORS/CORRECTIONS

*Error:* Right hand holds the club too much in the palm.

*Correction:* The club should be held more with the fingers. The club lies diagonally across the fingers with the joints of the second and third fingers on the club and the middle of the index finger touching the club. Review the grip procedure.

*Error:* Left hand holds the club with the butt end at the middle of the palm rather than placed under the fleshy part of the palm's heel.

*Correction:* The butt end should be under the fleshy part of the palm's heel. Hold the club in the left hand in front of you and parallel to the ground. If held correctly, it should be able to be held with the butt end under the fleshy part of the palm's heel and the first joint of the index finger (like gripping a pistol). Review the grip procedure.

*Error:* The clubface is not properly aligned when taking the grip or holding the club.

*Correction:* Before holding the club, place the clubface on the ground so the clubface is aligned parallel to the hands of a clock in the 12 o'clock position. The leading edge of the sole of the clubface must be perpendicular to the target line or form a 90-degree angle.

*Error:* Poor ball position.

*Correction:* Ball is placed in line with the left heel for a driver and at about the center of the stance, for short and mid irons.

*Error:* The distance from the ball is incorrect (too far or close).

*Correction:* The hands should fall just about over the toe line. The arms hang freely downward from the shoulders. Another check is that about a hand's width should be between the butt end of the club and the thighs.

# 3

# FULL-SWING BASICS

Your ability to understand how to execute the golf swing and the principles of how the components of the swing affect the flight of the ball is very important. Once you understand, you will begin to see why you make certain errors and how to correct them. The ball's flight has certain characteristics—such as how far it travels, how high or low (trajectory), and its direction. One of the important precursors to learning the golf swing is to see a good picture of it. It is then that you will begin to understand what moving the club is all about in the creation of a good swing.

Where do you use the full swing? First it is used from the teeing area on each hole to get the ball in play. If you are in a good position, your second shot on par 4s, and the second and third shot on par 5s will most likely be a full swing motion.

In this chapter, the full swing will be discussed in components for purposes of learning the motion. Each component of the swing may be practiced separately. However, the golfer must remember that the golf swing is a fluid, rhythmical movement. If you will think of the golf swing as a swing and not a hit at a ball, you will make good progress from the beginning.

## Learner Skills

1. Demonstrate the correct movement sequence of the full swing.
2. Execute a full swing with tempo and balance.
3. Recognize the nine shot patterns of the golf ball.
4. Describe the factors which affect ball flight.

## Prerequisite Skills

1. Knows the names of each club included in a full set.
2. Demonstrates an understanding of the set-up, including the grip, stance, posture, alignment, and ball position.

# THE FULL SWING

The golf swing is just that, a swing. In nearly all sports which involve swinging an implement such as a bat or racquet, the ball or object to be struck is moving most of the time. The player will need to alter the swing to meet the moving ball, as in tennis. However, in golf, the ball is always stationary. The golf swing is like most other swings, especially swinging a bat. In golf, you need to learn only one basic swing or smaller versions of it.

The golf swing is a circular motion, except the circle is at an angle, instead of horizontal, because the ball is on the ground. If you could put the ball on a tee that was chest high, swinging the golf club would be a lot like swinging a bat. The movement would be away from the ball, swinging around your lower body, back to the ball and through to your other side.

# FULL SWING BASICS

The golf swing has distinct phases. The first is preparing to swing or setting up to the ball (address). The second phase is the actual swing movement. The swing is completed in one smooth, fluid motion; however, for learning's sake, it will be broken into five parts—the take-away, backswing, downswing, forwardswing, and follow-through or finish.

## Take-Away and Backswing

Figure 3.1 illustrates the correct set-up or beginning. Remember this always: "Every good golf swing begins with a good set-up."

Observe that the first move, or take-away of the club backward, is a single unit move along the target line (Figure 3.2). The club moves on the target line until it is just past your right foot. This is essential to making a good backswing. It allows the club to be moved while staying connected to the body. The move should be low and slow. The butt end and the face of the club move together. You will see that the arms and shoulders form a triangle. Think of moving the triangle without it losing its shape. You should also be transferring your weight toward the right side. There are key thoughts about the swing movement that will help you to make the correct movement sequence.

- Move the club, hands, arms, and shoulders as a single unit.
- Move the club along the target line, away from the ball toward your stance line, as you coil the upper trunk around your spine, against your lower steady body. Note: The movement is like a gate or door opening on an angle. This creates a rotational move around the spine.
- The swing movement is <u>not</u> like a see-saw, where the shoulders tilt. The turn is against a stable lower body and around the angled spine established at address.

**FIGURE 3.1   Set-Up/Address**
A good swing begins with a
proper set-up.

**FIGURE 3.2   Take-Away.** Maintain the triangle formed by the
arms and shoulders.

- Your spine angle established at address should remain the same throughout the swing until the beginning of the follow-through.

## Waist High

Continue to move the club to waist high with the arms extended. Figure 3.3
illustrates the club position at waist high. It is parallel to the stance line. The
toe of the club points straight up. It is important that the toe point up, not to
the front or toward the rear. The back of your left hand should be positioned
as if you were shaking hands with someone standing at your right side.

## Shoulder High

As the arms and hands approach a shoulder-high position (Figure 3.4), the hips
have turned 45 degrees and the left shoulder points toward the ball, having
turned 90 degrees. There is good extension in the left arm while not being too
rigid. The idea is to coil the body to a position behind the ball. This is the
windup that will help create clubhead speed on the downswing, The coil is
completed against a braced right leg. The right foot is firmly on the ground with
the knee flexed.

**FIGURE 3.3  Backswing Waist High.** Toe of the club points to the sky. The left hand is held as if shaking hands with someone at your left side.

**FIGURE 3.4  Shoulder High.** At 10 o'clock, the wrists are fully hinged from a light grip and weight of the club.

## The Top

Figure 3.5 shows the club position and body posture at the top of the backswing. The club is near parallel. Some individuals are not flexible enough to take the club to parallel to the ground at the top. It is okay to not reach parallel.

The elbows are even with each other, which keeps the club parallel to the target line. The hands and club are above the right shoulder, with the left arm fairly straight but not rigid, and the right elbow points down (Figure 3.5). This produces a square clubface. Bending the left wrist toward the front produces an open clubface, resulting in a slice. Bending the wrist toward the back produces a closed clubface, resulting in a hook. The spine angle at the set-up has not changed its position. The right knee remains flexed and supports the coil of the body. At the top of the swing, your weight should be transferred to the inside of your right foot. Your head should be turned a little to the right and be behind the ball. It is important to coil behind the ball.

**FIGURE 3.5    At the Top.** Hands are at 11 o'clock. Shoulders are turned about 90 degrees. Hips are turned about 45 degrees.

**FIGURE 3.6    Downswing.** Right elbow drops close to the right side. Maintain a wrist hinge at the beginning of the downswing, which starts with a shift or change in weight to the left side, and then pull the club down with the arms.

## Downswing

Figure 3.6 illustrates the move from the top to start the downswing. Give yourself time to set the club at the top. Novices often rush this part of the swing. The downswing is initiated with the lower body by a shift of the weight toward the left side and bringing the left arm down with the right elbow moving toward your right hip. The hips start to rotate to the left side, allowing the arms and club to drop into the hitting zone at impact. At the waist-high position on the downswing, the club is at an angle to the left arm. This helps to make a strong impact. If the weight is transferred to the left side, the arms and hands will naturally follow. Think about swinging through the ball, not hitting at the ball. Think in terms of moving the club toward the target. Think swing!

## Impact

Figure 3.7 illustrates the club and body position near impact. At the moment of contact with the ball, the upper body remains a little more behind the ball than does the lower body. The arms are extended, with the clubface square, as it was at address. The weight is returning to the left side. The eyes are focused and the head is steady behind the ball. The left arm is straight and in line with the shaft of the club. Remember to accelerate through the ball, down the target line, as you are making a swing and not a hit.

## Forwardswing

After impact, the arms remain extended and continue to move the club down the target line, to inside, and back to waist high on the left side (Figure 3.8). It is important to continue the swing through the ball toward the target. This keeps the club accelerating through impact avoiding a "hit" at the ball. You also must rotate your hips toward the target. The right hand should be turned so that, if opened would be in a hand shake position. This takes the club to the

**FIGURE 3.7   Near Impact.** Eyes stay focused on the ball, and arms are fully extended as they were at address.

**FIGURE 3.8   Forward Swing— Post-Impact.** Club hand continues to move down the target line.

**FIGURE 3.9   Waist High (Forward Swing).** Right heel is off the ground as weight is transferred to the left side. The club is moved to the inside and parallel to the stance line (left side).

inside and parallel to the stance line (Figure 3.9). The body has turned toward the target, and the arms are extended with the toe of the club pointing straight up. This position mirrors the waist-high position on the backswing.

## Follow-Through (Finish)

Figures 3.10 and 3.11 illustrate the follow-through and completion of the swing. The key is balance, with the weight shifted to the left foot. The golfer has turned to face the target on the follow-through. The hands have moved to a point above the left shoulder with the club shaft behind your back. Visualize the finish of the swing with your weight on your left foot, with the right foot resting up on the toes, as you face the target. Hold the finish of the swing as if someone were going to take your picture. It is important to finish the swing with the upper body over the lower body facing the target. This keeps you from decelerating the swing at impact. The Full Swing Skill Builder Checklist (Figure 3.12) provides key points in the swing to achieve as you begin your first attempts and follow with practice.

**FIGURE 3.10**   Follow-Through

**FIGURE 3.11   Finish Position.**
Back is straight. Right foot is
balanced on the toes. Hands are
above the shoulders on the left
side. Body is balanced on the left
foot. Stomach faces the target.

Name _____    Score _____

**Posture and Alignment**
____ arms relaxed and extended, palms facing each other
____ feet apart, inside shoulder width
____ weight evenly distributed on balls of feet
____ stance line parallel to target line
____ upper torso leans forward, bending at hip joint; back straight
____ hips and shoulders parallel to target line

**Backswing**
____ shoulders begin to turn away from ball until left shoulder points behind ball
____ arms, hands, and club move away, inside target line to stance line, then upward
 as a single unit
____ hips turn to right about 45 degrees, left knee points behind ball
____ back points toward target
____ hands above right shoulder about ear height, wrists flexed, thumbs pointed
 toward target
____ heel of left foot slightly off the ground

*Continued*

**Downswing**

\_\_\_\_ weight shifts to left side or toward target, left heel returns to ground
\_\_\_\_ hips return to set-up position parallel to target line
\_\_\_\_ shoulders begin to follow hips and return to set-up position parallel to target line

**Impact**

\_\_\_\_ arms, hands move toward right hip and return to set-up position parallel to target line; arms straight
\_\_\_\_ weight shifts to left foot or toward target
\_\_\_\_ hips begin turn toward target

**Follow-Through**

\_\_\_\_ hips, shoulders, arms, hands continue to rotate toward target
\_\_\_\_ chest faces target
\_\_\_\_ arms, hands continue upward until ear height is reached, wrists flexed; club parallel or below
\_\_\_\_ weight totally on left foot or target side
\_\_\_\_ right foot—heel elevated, on toes with knee pointed toward target

Score = # of elements present while swinging from a set-up position, no ball.

Score Test #1 _____    Score Test #2 _____

**FIGURE 3.12    Full Swing Motion Skill Builder Checklist**

### Full Swing with Irons and Woods

Basically, the swing motion is the same with irons and woods. However, with short irons—pitching wedge, 9- and 8-irons, you will be closer to the ball, as these clubs are shorter than the long irons. The woods are longer than the irons, so with them you will be farther from the ball. With short and mid-irons, wedges, 9- and 8-irons, 7- and 6-irons, the ball is positioned at the center of your stance. Your stance will be just a bit narrower than shoulder width. With longer irons—5-, 4-, and 3-irons—and woods, the ball is in line with your left shirt pocket or just forward of center. With the driver, the ball is placed just inside the left heel. A shoulder-width stance should be used with long irons and woods.

## FACTORS AFFECTING THE BALL'S FLIGHT

The characteristics of ball flight include: direction, distance, and trajectory (how high the ball travels). There are five factors that affect the ball's flight: the speed of the clubhead at impact; hitting the clubface on the center, or sweet spot; how square the clubface is to the intended line of flight; the path on which the club is moved; and the angle of the clubhead as it contacts the ball.

### Directional Influences

The direction the ball travels is influenced by the path on which you swing the club and the clubhead position when it strikes the ball. The way in which you align your body has a significant impact on the direction the ball travels. Many ball flight errors or directional problems are based on poor alignment.

### Distance Influences

Distance is influenced by the speed at which the club is moved, how square the clubface is at impact, and the angle of approach as the club contacts the ball. A shallow angle produces a longer ball flight than a steep angle. Clubs are purposely designed to provide a different angle of approach to the ball. Short clubs (high numbered) (high loft) produce a high trajectory and shorter distances. Long clubs (low numbered) (low loft) produce a low trajectory and longer distances.

### Ball Flight Patterns/Directions

There are nine ball flight patterns based on either the swing path of the club, the clubface position at impact, or a combination of the two. Figure 3.13 illustrates the nine patterns of ball flight. Figure 3.14 illustrates the causes for each pattern.

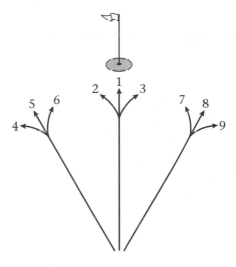

**FIGURE 3.13   Ball Flight Options**

| Ball Flight | Cause |
|---|---|
| Ball flies in a straight line toward the intended line of flight (straight shot). | Swing fundamentals correct—a square clubface and inside-to square-to inside swing path. |
| Ball moves to the left of the intended target (pull). | The club moves from outside the target line on the backswing; inside on the forwardswing and follow-through (outside to inside swing path), with the clubface square. |
| Ball moves to the right of the intended target (push). | The club moves from inside the target line on the backswing and downswing to outside the line on the forwardswing and follow-through (in to outside swing path with square clubface). |
| Ball moves straight to the intended target, then curves to the left (hook). | The club path was correct, but the face was closed at impact, imparting right to left spin on the ball. |
| Ball moves straight to the target but curves to the right (slice). | The club path was correct, but the face was open at impact, imparting right to left spin on the ball. |
| Ball moves to the left of the intended target, then curves to the right (pull-slice). | The club path was out to in, and the clubface was open at impact, imparting left to right spin on the ball. |
| Ball moves to the left of the intended target, then curves left (pull-hook). | The club path was outside to inside, and the clubface was closed at impact, imparting right to left spin on the ball. |
| Ball moves to the right of the intended target, then curves to the left (push-hook). | The club path was inside to outside, and the clubface was closed at impact, imparting right to left spin on the ball. |
| Ball moves to the right of the intended target, then curves to the right (push-slice). | The club path was inside to outside, and the clubface was open at impact, imparting left to right spin on the ball. |

**FIGURE 3.14    Ball Flight Paths and Causes**

1. *Straight path.* The swing path is inside-to square-to inside the target line. The clubface is square at impact. Figure 3.15 illustrates the set-up and swing path for the straight shot.
2. *Draw.* The swing path is inside-to square-to inside. The clubface is closed to the target line at impact. A draw is a ball that starts out straight, then curves slightly from right to left as a result of counterclockwise spin on the ball. A hook shot is like the draw except that the curvature of the ball is more to the left.
3. *Fade.* The swing path is inside-to square-to inside, with the clubface open at impact. A fade is a ball that starts out straight, then curves slightly from left to right as a result of clockwise spin on the ball. The slice is somewhat like the fade except that the curve is more to the right. The first three ball

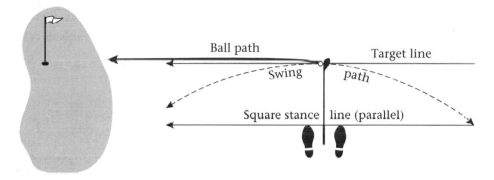

**FIGURE 3.15    Straight Shot**

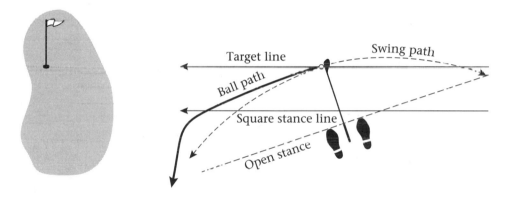

**FIGURE 3.16    Pull-Hook**

flight patterns are caused by the clubface position to the target line at impact. The swing path is the same for these patterns.

4. *Pull-Hook.* The swing path is outside to inside the target line. The clubface is closed at impact. Figure 3.16 demonstrates the set-up and swing path for a pull-hook shot.

5. *Pull.* The swing path is outside to inside the target line. The clubface is square at impact. The ball travels to the left and straight. Figure 3.17 illustrates the pull shot.

6. *Pull-Slice.* The swing path is outside to inside the target line. The clubface is open at impact. The ball travels straight left, initially, and then curves to the right. Figure 3.18 illustrates the set-up and swing path for a pull-slice shot pattern.

7. *Push-Hook.* The swing path is inside to outside the target line. The clubface is closed at impact. The ball travels straight right, initially, and then curves to the left. Figure 3.19 includes the set-up, swing path, and clubface position at impact for a push-hook and a push-slice.

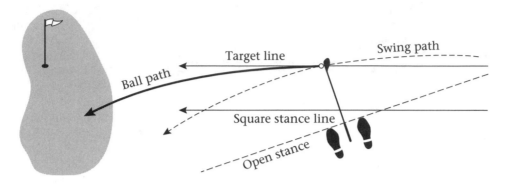

**FIGURE 3.17   Pull Shot**

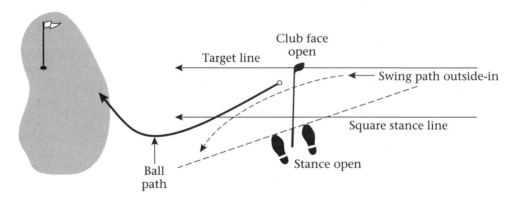

**FIGURE 3.18   Pull-Slice**

8. *Push.* The swing path is inside to outside the target line. The clubface is square at impact (Figure 3.20). The ball travels to the right in a straight path.
9. *Push-Slice.* The swing path is inside to outside the target line. The clubface is open at impact. The ball travels straight to the right initially, then curves to the right. See Figure 3.19.

Patterns such as pull-hooks and pull-slices are caused by swing paths that are outside to inside the target line and a closed or open clubface at impact. Patterns such as push-hooks and push-slices are caused by inside to outside swing paths and a closed or open clubface at impact. Poor alignment, such as closed or open stances, contribute to swing path errors.

A parallel inside path is depicted in Figure 3.15. This is the path needed on the backswing and forwardswing to hit a straight shot, provided the clubface is square at impact.

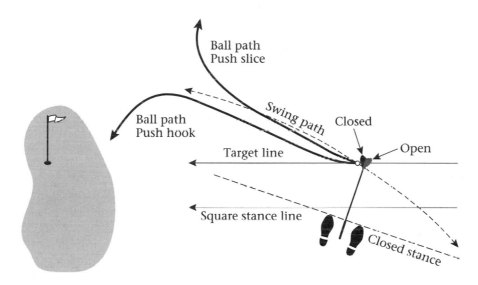

**FIGURE 3.19　Push-Slice/Push-Hook**

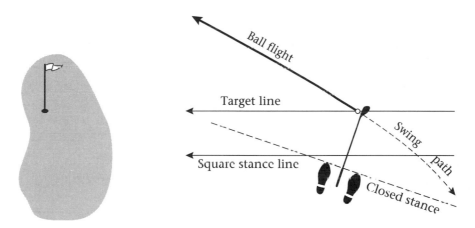

**FIGURE 3.20　Push Shot**

An open clubface results in left to right spin on the ball, causing it to slice or fade to the right. A closed clubface results in right to left spin on the ball, causing it to draw or hook. Figures 3.21 and 3.22 provide illustrations of an open and closed clubface.

Some golf instructors refer to these as ball flight errors. In some instances, it may be necessary to draw or fade the ball around an obstacle or dogleg in the fairway. These patterns are not always errors. They may be intentional to meet the need for the shot. As you progress from a beginner to a more advanced player, you will want to learn how to intentionally hook, draw, fade, and slice the ball.

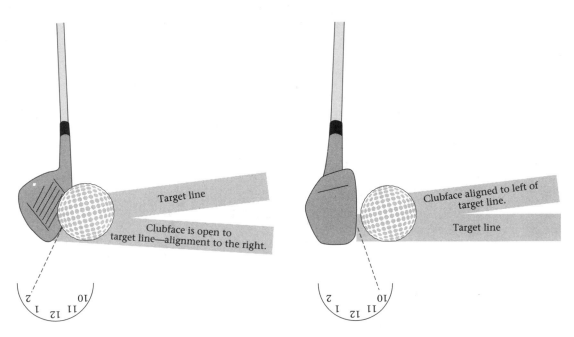

**FIGURE 3.21   Open Clubface.** Club's toe points to 2 o'clock instead of 12 o'clock. Clubface is open to target line—alignment to the right.

**FIGURE 3.22   Closed Clubface.** Club's toe points to 10 o'clock instead of 12 o'clock. Clubface aligned to left of target line.

---

**Full Swing Skill Builders**

ATHLETIC STANCE DRILL

*Purpose:* Feel the athletic stance and weight transfer in the golf swing.

*Equipment:* full-length mirror

*Activity:* Review the correct stance and posture for the set-up. Assume the athletic stance. Transfer your weight to the right foot, then to the left foot. Do so until you can do this smoothly and easily while maintaining the same posture. Avoid swaying and rolling your ankles. Pretend you are throwing a ball sidearmed. Think how you transferred your weight as you threw a ball. Pretend you are making a sidearm throw.

BASEBALL DRILL

*Purpose:* Experience weight shift and body coil.

*Equipment:* 7- or 8-irons

*Activity:*

1. Set up to an imaginary ball. Grip the club and raise it to a horizontal position just above your waist. Make a full turn to the right by rotating your shoulders and transferring your weight to the inside of your right foot. Move your weight back to the left and uncoil the upper body to the left as if to strike a baseball pitched just above your waist.
2. Focus on keeping your shoulders level and your knees flexed.
3. Note how the level shoulder turn helps to coil the upper body against the lower body. Have a partner watch you, then take a turn.
   Score = # of swings made with shoulders level and body balanced: ____

## HALF SWING DRILL

*Purpose:* Feel the arms, hands, and club moving as a unit and weight transfer.

*Equipment:* 9- or 8-irons

*Activity A:*

1. Begin the activity first without clubs. Set up to an imaginary golf ball as if you were going to swing. Put your palms together. Turn your shoulders and arms together to a position at waist high on the right side. Allow your weight to transfer. Pretend someone is there, and you are shaking hands with both hands.
2. Move your weight back to the left side, and move your arms and hands to waist high on the left side and hold. Your hands should be parallel to your target line and stance line. Imagine shaking hands with someone on the left side. Repeat this movement until you are able to do it smoothly.

Score = # of swings made with your hands in the correct position: _____

*Activity B:* Repeat the above activity with a club in your hands. Take the normal grip. At waist high, on both sides, the toe of the club should point straight up to the sky. Note that you have to cross the left hand over the right hand as you move to the right side waist high. Cross the right hand over the left as you swing back to waist high on the left side. Repeat this activity with your hands about 4 inches apart on the grip.

Score = # of swings made with the toe of clubhead pointing straight up: _____

## THREE-QUARTER SWING DRILL

1. Repeat the same drill above except swing to a three-quarter position on the backswing and forwardswing. So you will move your arms and hands to shoulder high on each side.
2. Your wrists will hinge to allow the club to move just beyond 90 degrees to your arms. The right arm will bend instead of staying straight, as you swing to shoulder high to the right. On the forward swing, the left arm will bend slightly as you reach shoulder high on the left side.
3. Swing shoulder high to shoulder high until you can do it smoothly, keeping your balance with each swing. Note that your hands will be at about 10 o'clock and 2 o'clock if a clock was behind you as you swing.

*Continued*

*Continued*

## FULL SWING WITHOUT A BALL

*Purpose:* To feel the motion of the full swing with balance and tempo.

*Equipment:* none for part A; 9-iron for part B; 5-iron and 3-wood for part C

*Activity A:*

1. Assume the set-up position to a ball with hands together. In slow motion, move the hands and arms to the take-away position; to above waist high (thumbs point to sky, wrists are hinged); then to the top; with your back pointing toward the target.
2. Start the downswing by moving your weight toward the left side; arms are straight at impact; the right heel is off the ground. Continue to waist high on the left side; thumbs should point to the target. Continue to the finish; hands should be head high with thumbs pointed to the rear. Hold the finish position as if someone were going to take your picture. Your stomach should face the target.
3. Check each position: take-away, waist-high backswing; three-quarter swing; top of backswing; weight shift to start downswing; impact; waist high to the left side (forwardswing); and the finish position.
4. Make ten swings, checking each position.

*Activity B:*

1. Repeat activity A, using an iron, moving in slow motion.
2. Repeat the activity, moving with tempo and balance.

*Activity C:*

1. Repeat the swing first in slow motion with a 5-iron, then a 3-wood.
2. Repeat the swing at a regular tempo and speed with the 5-iron and 3-wood.

*Activity D:*

1. Place your feet together and make a full swing. Note how your weight transfers to the right, then back to the left side. Repeat this ten times.
2. Make a full swing with your feet about shoulder width apart. As you finish the swing, step forward with your right foot as if taking a step.

## FULL SWING WITH A BALL

*Purpose:* To feel solid contact with the club to the ball.

*Equipment:* 9-iron, 5-iron, 3- or 5-wood, tees, golf balls

*Activity A:*

1. Set up to a ball. The ball should be in the center of your stance on a low tee if you do not have a good lie. Make two practice swings, brushing the turf each time. Make a full swing with the 9-iron, contact the ball, and finish your swing. Key thought: Pretend you are making a practice swing with the ball in position. Concentrate on making solid contact with the center of the clubface on the ball as you swing through the ball to the finish position.
2. Repeat the procedure swinging the 5-iron and 3- or 5-wood. For the woods, place the ball just forward of center, on a tee.

*Activity B:*

Make full swings with the ball, using five balls. Determine how far each ball travels. Average the distance. Repeat for each club  pitching wedge, 9 iron, 8 iron, 7 iron, 6-iron, 5-iron, 5-wood, 3-wood. Record the distance hit with each club.

*Activity C:*

With a partner, see who can be the most accurate with a pitching wedge from 20, 30, 40, and 50 yards; with a 9-iron from 60, 70, and 80 yards.

## FULL SWING WITH DRIVER

*Purpose:* To feel the full swing motion using a driver.

*Equipment:* twenty golf balls for each person, driver, tees

*Activity:*

1. Set up and align your body to a selected target. The ball should be placed just inside your left foot, a couple of inches inside the left heel. The ball should be teed so one-half of the ball is above the face of the driver. Take two practice swings before making the actual swing. Make a smooth full swing, impacting the ball, and continue to the finish position.
2. Key thoughts: Swing smooth, not fast; swing through the ball and continue to the finish position.

## COMMON ERRORS AND CORRECTIONS

*Error:* Aligns body incorrectly to the target. This causes the ball to land left or right of the target.

*Correction:* Review the alignment procedure using the parallel lines or railroad tracks. Practice alignment with two clubs or yardsticks on the ground, placed for the target and stance lines. Practice alignment without a yardstick, selecting an intermediate target. Have someone check your alignment by placing a yardstick or club on the ground next to your toes.

*Error:* Ball is placed in the wrong position in the stance.

*Correction:* Set up with a club. Make two or three practice swings contacting the ground. Note where the divot is. Place the ball at that position. It should be near the center of the stance for short and mid-irons, or just forward of center for woods and long irons.

*Error:* Sets up too far or too close to the ball.

*Correction:* Set up to the ball with a club. Release the club. If your hands fall backward, you are too far from the ball; if they fall forward, you are too close to the ball. You should be able to pass a hand between the end of the grip and your body without touching either. Your hands should be positioned just outside your toe line.

*Error:* Decelerates the club through impact and does not finish the swing.

*Correction:* Think of a roller coaster building up speed as it starts down the track. Concentrate on swinging the club and not on hitting the ball. Swing and hold the finish position. Take a step forward as you finish the swing.

*Error:* Takes the clubface back closed.

*Continued*

*Continued*

*Correction:* Take the club back with the grip end and face together. The toe of the club should turn right and point to the sky at waist high.

*Error:* Moves the club too far inside on the backswing.

*Correction:* Start the backswing with the butt end of the club moving to your right thigh, as you move it toward your stance line. Do not take the clubhead first to the stance line as this will lead to taking it too far inside.

*Error:* Takes the club back toward the target line or outside and makes an outside to inside swing path.

*Correction:* Take the club to parallel to the stance line as you swing to the top. Be sure to make a good body turn with the left shoulder under the chin. Alignment should be square.

*Error:* Picks the club up from the soled position too quickly.

*Correction:* Move the club, arms, and chest together in a low take-away.

*Error:* Moves the club with the arms and hands only and does not turn the trunk.

*Correction:* Set up to the ball and turn to look at a person standing behind you. Your left knee should point toward the ball.

*Error:* Weight remains on the left side or does not shift to the right side on backswing.

*Correction:* Turn your head slightly to the right as you rotate your left shoulder under your chin. Pick up your left foot. If you cannot pick up your left foot, you have not shifted your weight. Or as you turn to the right, pick up your left foot, then as you turn back to the left, pick up your right foot.

*Error:* Hit on top or near the top of the ball. Misses the ball.

*Correction:* Arms should extend on the downswing. Maintain through impact the posture established at address.

# 4

# PUTTING

The putt (Figure 4.1) is a stroke intended to roll the golf ball to the cup along the green or putting surface. During a round of golf, the putting stroke is used 43 percent of the time if a score of par for the eighteen holes is achieved. Therefore, putting is the most frequently used stroke in a round of play and should be given a lot of practice time.

To become a good putter, you will need to develop the following basic skills: (1) a consistent pre-shot routine; (2) a correct and comfortable grip; (3) proper set-up over the ball; (4) a mechanically correct and repeatable stroke; (5) the ability to read the greens; (6) confidence in your ability to send the ball into the hole.

## Learner Skills

1. Demonstrate a correct grip for putting.
2. Demonstrate a pre-shot routine.
3. Demonstrate proper set-up for executing the putt.
4. Execute a mechanically sound putting stroke.
5. When asked to determine the line of putt, correctly identify the direction of the break.

## Prerequisite Skills

1. Understands the terms *grip, stance, alignment, target line, stance line.*

**FIGURE 4.1    The Putt**

## *PUTTING FUNDAMENTALS*

### *Grip*

**Reverse Overlap.**    This is the most common grip. The putter is held with the palms facing each other and the thumbs placed on top of the grip. The front side of the grip on the putter is flat. Figure 4.2 illustrates the reverse overlap grip. Grip the putter lightly to prevent tension in the arms and hands. Tension can ruin tempo or how smoothly and rhythmically you move the putter on the backswing and follow-through.

**Left Hand.**    Grip the putter with the left hand at the top of the shaft with mostly the last three fingers. The thumb is placed on top of the grip. The index finger of the left hand is placed over the last three fingers of the right hand.

**Right Hand.**    Grip the putter shaft with mostly the last three fingers with the thumb on top. Both hands should be close together, as they need to work as a unit.

Your shoulders, arms, and hands must feel relaxed and hang naturally. Your elbows should be close to your body.

**FIGURE 4.2 Reverse Overlap Grip—Front View.** "Vs" formed by thumbs. Index fingers point toward the left and right shoulders rather than parallel as in regular grip.

## Stance

There are any number of ways that professional players assume their putting stance. Beginners should start out with a square stance, with the feet spread slightly narrower than the shoulders, about 12 to 18 inches apart. However, golfers tend to develop whatever stance is comfortable to them. It is really an individual thing.

Figure 4.3 illustrates a basic set-up for putting. Within this range, it is important to find a stance that feels balanced and comfortable to you. Experiment, taking your stance with different widths between your feet. Your weight should be about evenly distributed, but some players prefer to have a little more weight on the left foot. The rest of your body, especially hips, shoulders, and legs, should be parallel to the target line.

## Posture

Your eyes should be over the target line or a little behind the ball. To accomplish this, flex your knees slightly and bend at the hips. If you held a yardstick

**FIGURE 4.3   Set-Up Putt.**
Hands are over the ball or just
in front of it. Weight is shifted a
bit more on the left side. Ball is
positioned forward of center
inside the left heel.

or your putter parallel to the ground across the bridge of your nose, it should
be parallel to the target line (Figure 4.3).

## Ball Position

Ideally, the putter face needs to contact the ball at the bottom of the swing
arc or slightly on the upswing. Generally, the ball should be positioned slightly
forward in the stance just inside the left foot (Figure 4.3). The hands should
be just slightly ahead of the ball. Do not set up with your hands behind the
ball.

## EXECUTION

### Set-Up

Address the ball after having decided on the line of putt from behind the ball (Figure 4.4). Feel confident that you can make the putt.

### Backswing

Take the putter back low to the ground, moving it with your shoulders, arms, and hands as one unit in a pendulum-style movement. Your lower body and head remain still (Figure 4.5). Any movement of the head, swaying of the body, or turning of the shoulders will likely pull the putter off line and cause the putt to be missed or minimize solid contact with the ball. Movement of the body other than the shoulders, arms, and hands may result in contacting the ball with the heel or toe of the putter.

After judging the distance of the putt, you should be able to determine how long a backswing to make. A backswing that is too long for the distance causes

**FIGURE 4.4    Ready to Swing—**
Set-Up

**FIGURE 4.5   Backswing.** On short putts, the putter moves back on a straight line.

**FIGURE 4.6   Impact.** At impact, the hands remain ahead of the ball.

you to subconsciously decelerate the putter as it approaches the ball. Deceleration as the club approaches the ball is a disaster to any golf swing.

## Impact

The putter head needs to be square (at a right angle) to the target line when the ball is contacted. The ball should be contacted on the sweet spot of the putter face. You must be focused on the ball with your head remaining still even shortly after impact (Figure 4.6). Keep the angle of the wrists and forearms fairly constant. You want to avoid a wrist bend at contact.

## Follow-Through

Keep the putter head moving down the target line. On all putts except short ones, the putter will naturally swing a little to the inside of the target line on the follow-through. Accelerate the putter through the ball at a good tempo (Figure 4.7).

**FIGURE 4.7   Follow-Through.**
Wrists are firm throughout the
swing. Head is still even after
impact.

## Mechanically Sound Stroke

The idea of putting is to create a good roll of the ball. The following elements
are present in a putting stroke that is mechanically sound.

- Set up in the correct posture and square to the target line.
- Keep your eyes focused on the spot where the ball is positioned until after
  you have made contact.
- Take the putter straight back on short putts and slightly inside the target
  line on longer putts. The stroke has a natural arc to it.
- Keep your eyes focused on the ball as you contact it and after accelerating
  through the ball (Figures 4.6 and 4.7). Keep the left wrist firm throughout
  acceleration on short and medium-length putts.
- Always accelerate the putter head through the ball along the target line
  (Figure 4.7).
- Develop a consistent pre-shot routine that you use on every putt.
- The stroke must be smooth with constant tempo.

The shoulders, arms, and hands move as a unit in a pendulum motion. The head and body should be still. Strive for a good smooth stroke, not a jab at the ball. Keep the putter moving through the ball toward the target. Even on long putts, strive for a good tempo or smooth stroke. On longer putts, the backswing will be longer but still smooth. On longer putts, your wrists will bend a little. This is okay. The ball needs to be hit firmly enough so that if it misses the hole it stops about 17 or 18 inches past the hole.

## Putting Pre-Shot Routine

All shots in golf should be preceded with a good pre-shot routine. The systematic steps in your putting routine should include the following: (1) read the green, (2) select a target, (3) address or set up, (4) note the distance, take a practice swing, (5) visualize the ball going into the cup, (6) feel confident you can make the putt, and (7) execute the swing. Figure 4.8 provides you with a Putting Skill Builder Checklist.

**Address**

____ stance narrower than shoulders
____ weight evenly distributed or slightly more on target foot
____ ball positioned target side of center (inside left heel)
____ hands are just ahead of ball
____ eyes over target line or just behind ball
____ hips, feet, shoulders square to target line
____ putter face square to target line
____ putter held in palms, thumbs on top of grip

**Execution**

____ wrists firm
____ head remains still prior to contact with ball
____ lower body remains still
____ backswing and forwardswing equal in length (forwardswing may be a little longer)
____ arms, hands, shoulders swing together
____ putter face square to target
____ stroke is smooth (pendulum motion)

**Comments:**

**FIGURE 4.8   Putting Skill Builder Checklist**

**Putting Skill Builders**

GRIP DRILL

*Purpose:* To develop an automatic, correct, and repeatable grip on the putter.

*Equipment:* putter and Putting Skill Builder Checklist

*Activity:*

1. One partner selects a putter. Face each other and describe to your partner how each hand is to be placed on the club. Have your partner check your hand position with the checklist.
2. Repeat the grip ten times without describing the hand positions. Have your partner repeat the procedure.

   *Alternative Activities*

3. You should also try this drill at home in front of a mirror. Practice the grip while watching television, especially a golf tournament.

*Evaluation:* Were you able to describe the correct hand position? Are you able to correctly grip the putter easily and automatically?

Score = the # of grips out of ten taken easily and correctly without assistance: _____

SWING LENGTH/SWING PATH DRILL

*Purpose:* To develop a consistent putting backswing and follow-through.

*Equipment:* putter and yardstick

*Activity:*

1. Place the yardstick in front of you, parallel to your feet. Stand with your feet about 1 foot apart about 10 inches from the yardstick. Grip the putter and rest the head on the middle of the yardstick. Practice bringing the clubhead straight back about 5 inches, then straight through 5 inches beyond the center. Repeat the swing, moving a few more inches back and through. Continue this until you can do the swing consistently and rhythmically.
2. Try this procedure moving from 8 inches back and 8 inches forward of the center. Repeat the back and through stroke, increasing the distance each time. Keep your head still and eyes focused on the center. Keep the putter head low and close to the yardstick. Swing from the shoulders, making a good pendulum stroke.
3. Take the putter back about a foot, then through the same length. The putter will move a little to the inside on the way back and inside on the way through with a longer-length stroke.

   *Alternative Activities*

4. This drill can be practiced almost anywhere, using a taped line or yardstick, even lines on the floor. Place two clubs parallel to each other about one-half inch wider than the length of the putter head. Practice taking the putter back and through without touching either club.

Score = the # of short smooth swings made correctly out of ten: _____

the # of long smooth swings made correctly out of ten: _____

*Continued*

*Continued*

## SOLID CONTACT DRILL

*Purpose:* Feel the solid contact with the ball on the sweet spot of the putter.

*Equipment:* putter and ten golf balls

*Activity:*

1. Find the sweet spot or center of balance of the putter head. Hold the putter vertically about 6 inches from the butt end with your index finger and thumb. Tap the toe end of the putter with your other index finger. The putter head should turn off-center.
2. Now tap the heel end of the putter with your finger. The putter head should turn off-center again. Tap the putter as near the center as you can. Continue tapping or poking with your index finger until you find the spot where the putter head does not turn off-center. This will be the sweet spot and the point where contact should be made with the ball.
3. Most putters have the sweet spot marked with a line or dot. If yours does not have it marked, place a piece of tape at the point you have identified as the sweet spot.
4. Take the correct putting stance, using correct posture, weight distribution, and placement of a ball in your stance. Next, align the putter face with the sweet spot at the center of the ball. Make a short swing about 5 to 8 inches back and 5 to 8 inches through, contacting the ball with the sweet spot.
5. Repeat this for all ten balls.
6. Then repeat the procedure with a longer backswing of 8 to 12 inches. Note how the putter feels and sounds at it contacts the ball with the sweet spot.

*Evaluation:*

Did the putter sound differently when hit on the sweet spot than it did off the sweet spot?
How does the ball roll when contacted with the sweet spot?
How does the ball roll when contacted with the toe or heel of the putter?

## SHORT PUTT DRILL

*Purpose:* Learn to firm the short putt and experience initial success.

*Equipment:* putter and ten balls, putting green (outdoors), or carpet and putting cup for indoors

*Activity:* Mark distances of 2 and 3 feet on one or four sides of the cup. Putt ten balls from each marker. Check the following points: smooth stroke; wrists firm; follow-through with the putter head on the target line; correct length for backswing and follow-through; body still, eyes over the target line or slightly behind and the head kept still until after the ball is contacted.

*Tips:* Stroke the ball to get it to the back edge of the hole, not the front. Putts of 3 feet or less should not be played outside the cup unless there is a severe break.

*Alternative Activity:* Repeat this drill, putting with your eyes closed. Listen for the ball to drop in the cup.

*Evaluation:*

Putts made with a smooth stroke: _____

Number of putts that went long: _____

Number of putts that were short: _____

Number of putts to the right: _____ to the left: _____

What are aspects of the short putt that you need to practice?

## FIVE-IN-A-ROW DRILL

*Purpose:* To develop consistency and success on short putts.

*Equipment:* putter and five golf balls

*Activity:*

1. Place the first ball 2 feet from the cup, then place the remaining four balls at 1-foot intervals behind the first ball. The balls should be placed where there is no break. Take your time, set up, and putt the first ball, then the second, third, and so on until all balls have been holed. If you miss, start over with the first ball.

   *Alternative Activity:*

2. Practice until you are able to hole three balls in a row.
3. Putt each ball with your eyes shut.
4. Putt looking at the hole.

## DISTANCE FEEL DRILL

*Purpose:* To learn the "feel" for distance.

*Equipment:* putter, ten golf balls, and tees

*Activity:*

1. Place a tee at each distance: 10, 15, 20, 25, 30 feet from a spot on the green. From that point, putt all ten balls to the first tee, then all ten to the second, and so forth. Concentrate on the feel and the length stroke needed to get the ball that distance.
2. Try a 10- or 15-foot putt with your eyes closed. The point is to get a "feel" for the distance. Do not putt at a hole in this drill.

Score = the # of putts out of ten at each distance: _____

## LAG IT DRILL

*Purpose:* Get the ball close to the cup so that a short second putt remains.

*Equipment:* putter, ten golf balls, and tees

*Activity:*

1. Begin putting from the 15-foot length. The idea is to land the ball within 1 or 2 feet of the cup, on either side, so that a second short putt is all that is left. This helps reduce the amount of three putts during a round of golf. The ball should stop within 2 feet past the hole.
2. After five of ten balls have stopped at the specified distance, increase the distance to be putted by 5 feet.

*Evaluation:*

How many putts were short? _____

What distance were the majority of putts falling short? _____

Falling longs (more than 2 feet)? _____

How many balls out of ten stopped within 2 feet past the hole at each distance? _____

## READING THE GREENS

"Reading the green" means to determine which way the ball will break or curve as it rolls toward the hole. This means determining the slope of the green and the speed. There are several factors that affect the way the ball will curve, or not curve, as it rolls toward the cup. Gravity affects the way the ball will curve and is most profound when the ball slows down. It will also affect the curve or "break" on a sidehill putt.

Physical factors such as mountains and water—streams, lakes, bays, oceans—affect the break. Generally, the ball will break toward the water. Where mountains are present, the putt is affected by gravity pulling the ball down the mountain. Visualize throwing a bucket of water onto the green and seeing which way the water flows. This gives you an idea of the break or which way the ball will curve. Figures 4.9 and 4.10 illustrate how the ball will break in different situations. Figure 4.9 illustrates a left to right break; Figure 4.10 illustrates a right to left break.

**FIGURE 4.9  Left to Right Break**

**FIGURE 4.10   Right to Left Break**

On longer putts, you should select an intermediate target on which to align the putter head just as you would in a full swing. When there is a break in the green, the target will not be the hole. In Figure 4.9, the putter will be directed at the point where the ball will begin its curve. Until that point, the putt is relatively straight. Speed will affect how much the ball breaks. If you putt the ball too hard, it will roll through the break. If you putt too soft, the ball will not hold the line and will break sooner than needed.

The type of grass used in the green may have an effect on the break. Bermuda grass, used often in hotter climates, will have the most impact on the break. If you are putting against the direction of the grain, the putt will move slower. Look at the grain from behind the ball. If it is dark, you will be putting against it. If it is shiny, you will be putting with the grain, and the ball will move faster. If you are putting to the side of the grain, the putt will break as if there were a slope in the direction the grain is growing. Generally, the grain grows toward the setting sun.

Weather conditions will affect the pace or speed of the greens, which in turn can also affect the break. If greens are wet from rain or morning dew, they will be slower than when they are dry. Conditions can change during a round of play. It may be hot and dry during play on the front of the course, but a sudden shower can make the greens slower during play on the back nine holes. Very wet greens will not break as much as when they are dry.

Very windy conditions can affect the roll of the ball, as well as an individual's stability while setting up over the putt. It helps to take a wider stance when putting during windy conditions.

Greens that have just been mowed will be faster than greens not recently mowed. The length of your putting stroke needs to be shortened on fast greens and lengthened on slow greens, while considering the distance of the putt.

### How to Read the Green

Start reading the green on an unfamiliar course when you get to the pro shop. Ask the professional or other staff members about the greens. They can tell you the type of grass used and any other specifics which might affect the putt.

The next step to reading the greens is to do so before you hit your approach shot. Although this is not always the case, you might want your approach shot to land below the cup if the green is sloped severely uphill. This way you can avoid a more difficult downhill putt. As you approach the green, note which way it slopes—to the right, left, uphill, downhill, or combinations of these. A green might slope uphill and to the right, for example.

On the green, stand a few feet behind the ball and look toward the ball and to the cup. Note if there is any break. As others in your group are putting, observe what the ball does if the other person's putt is near or on your line. This will give you the idea about the break and the speed of the green.

## Reading the Greens Skill Builders

DETERMINE THE LINE DRILL

*Purpose:* Recognize the slope and break of a putt.

*Equipment:* putter and five golf balls per pair

*Activity:*

1. Select holes on a practice green that will have a break to them. Designate reading and putting points on the green by marking them with a tee. These points should be about 10 to 20 feet from the cup and be on a line with a break.
2. Stand behind the ball about 5 feet and try to determine the line of the putt or the break. A verbal description of the line should be given: in other words, say to yourself, "The break is right to left about six inches." Then note a spot on the green to putt the ball. This will be the line of the putt that is straight. The break takes more effect when the putt slows down. Continue putting, making corrections after each putt.

PRE-SHOT ROUTINE DRILL

*Purpose:* To develop a consistent pre-shot routine for putting.

*Equipment:* putter and five balls

*Activity:* Place a ball 7 to 10 feet from the cup. Review the steps for a pre-shot routine. Practice the pre-shot routine for putting. Individualize the routine for yourself. Putt twenty times using the routine you have developed.

COMMON PUTTING ERRORS AND
CORRECTIONS

*Error:* Decelerates the putter as it approaches the ball

*Correction:* Practice the Swing Length Drill. Deceleration is usually caused by too long a backswing. Putt from 3 feet with little backswing, pushing the ball to the hole. Think of these images; driving a nail through the ball with the putter, and the putter traveling down the line toward the target.

*Error:* Pulls the ball to the left of the target. Aligns incorrectly, shoulders open to target. Turns shoulders to the left during stroke. Uses an outside to inside swing path.

*Correction:* Practice the alignment procedure described for putting in this chapter. Pulling the ball is a result of an outside to inside swing path of the putter head, usually resulting from an open stance or alignment to the left.

*Error:* Pushes the ball to the right of the target.

*Correction:* Practice the Swing Length/Swing Path Drill. A pushed putt results mainly from a closed stance. This may cause the putter to be moved inside to outside the putting line unless you are able to compensate. Practice with a square stance, taking the club back and through on the correct swing path.

*Error:* Hands are placed too far ahead of the ball, hooding the clubface, causing the ball to hop or jump before it begins to roll.

*Correction:* Check for proper ball placement in the stance. Your hands should be just slightly ahead of the ball.

*Error:* Moves head toward cup as stroke is made; usually wants to see if the ball is going into the cup.

*Correction:* Putt ten balls from 3 feet listening for the ball to drop into the cup. Focus on the front of the ball as the stroke is made. Count to two before looking at the cup after the stroke is made.

## PUTTING PROCEDURES

1. If more than one person is playing, the ball farthest from the hole is putted first, then the next farthest one. The ball closest to the hole is putted last. If you are in someone's line and closer to the hole, you may elect to putt out or choose to mark your ball.
2. If you are on the green and putting, the flagstick or pin must be attended by another person or removed. If you putt from on the green and hit the flagstick, it is a two-stroke penalty in stroke play and loss of the hole in match play. Stand to the side and hold the flag and the stick with one hand. Stand to a side that does not create a shadow over the line of putt. After the ball is in motion, remove the flagstick and lay it out of the way of other putts, unless someone else needs it attended.
3. Once the ball is on the putting green, it may be marked with a coin or other marker, lifted, and cleaned. The marker is placed behind the golf ball.
4. Loose impediments, such as sand, leaves, pine needles, etc., may be removed or brushed aside.
5. Ball marks or old hole plugs may be repaired.
6. The putting surface may not be tested by rubbing the surface or rolling a ball over it.
7. A player shall not stand astride the line of putt or an extension of the line behind the ball, nor should either foot touch the line.
8. During stroke play, when your ball is on the green and it touches another player's ball on the green, it is a two-stroke penalty. The other player's ball must be replaced.
9. After all have putted out, the flagstick must be replaced in the cup. All should move off the green toward the next tee without delay.

## *Practice Evaluation*

Putting requires dedication to practicing. As you practice the drills, make a mental note of your successes and the things on which you need to work.

| | | | |
|---|---|---|---|
| Alignment: | ____ good | ____ fair | ____ needs work |
| Posture: | ____ good | ____ fair | ____ needs work |
| Grip: | ____ good | ____ fair | ____ needs work |
| Stroke: | ____ good tempo | ____ fair tempo | ____ needs work |

Comments:

# 5

# CHIPPING

Chipping is part of the short game of golf. The basic chip shot is used most often when the player is around or near the green. The main idea of the chip shot is to carry the ball low, have it land just onto the green, and roll to the hole. Situations where the chip shot would be used are depicted in Figures 5.1A and B. The ball lies about 5 yards from the edge of the green, and there is about 35 feet of green between the ball and the hole. You may be close to the edge of the green but unable to putt because of the terrain being too rough or thick.

**FIGURE 5.1A** Where Chip Shot is Needed

**FIGURE 5.1B** Where Chip Shot is Needed

It is much more accurate to chip the ball and let it land a few feet onto the green and roll to the hole than to try to pitch it with a wedge. The chip shot is mostly a one-lever swing with little wrist action. So there is less room for error when making the chip shot versus other shots. In many situations, lower-lofted clubs such as the 6-, 7-, or 8-irons are used, as they create more roll and send the ball low if there is ample green available. Chipping requires some practice to master, but it will be a real stroke saver around the greens, taking pressure off putting. This shot helps the golfer get the ball close to the hole for a one-putt, in many cases to save par.

## Learner Skills

1. Explain the circumstances that would indicate the use of the chip shot.
2. Describe the elements of the chip shot related to address and execution.
3. Demonstrate the correct set-up and swing motion for the basic chip shot.

## Prerequisite Skills

1. Understands the concepts of grip, stance, ball position, weight distribution, and posture.
2. Understands the concept of club loft.
3. Understands the concepts of target and stance lines.

# CHIP SHOT FUNDAMENTALS

## Set-Up and Swing Motion

### Address/Set-Up

*Grip:*   Take a regular grip, gripping slightly down on the club. Your hands should be positioned with the club grip near your left thigh and a little forward of the ball.

*Stance:*   The stance is slightly open and narrower than the shoulders. The shoulders are square to the target line with the hips slightly open. This allows room to swing the club on the target line.

*Posture:*   To establish the correct posture over the ball, bend slightly forward at the hips, and flex the knees a bit. Your back should be straight.

*Ball Position:*   The ball is placed at the center of your stance and closer to your toes than it would be for a full swing. Some instructors recommend that the ball be placed toward the rear of center.

**FIGURE 5.2 Set-Up.** Stand closer to the ball as in the putt. Hands are near the left thigh.

*Weight Distribution:* Your weight should be more on your left foot or shifted toward the target.

*Club Position:* The leading edge of the face is square to the target line.

**Execution.** Find a landing spot. The landing spot depends on the club you are using and the distance to the hole. The lower the loft, the closer to the edge of the green will be the landing spot. From there, the ball should roll close to the hole.

What club should you choose? It depends on the distance to the hole, how far you are from the green, and the slope of the green. As a general guideline, you need to consider the amount of air time and roll that the club will create and how much green is available. Figure 5.3 illustrates the air time and landing spots for specific clubs. It is recommended that you learn to use a variety of clubs for chipping so you will not have to alter your swing as you would if using the same club all of the time.

Longer chip shots will require that you bend your right wrist a little. Just sweep the club back low to the ground. The distance you take the club back depends on how far the ball needs to travel and on the club you are using.

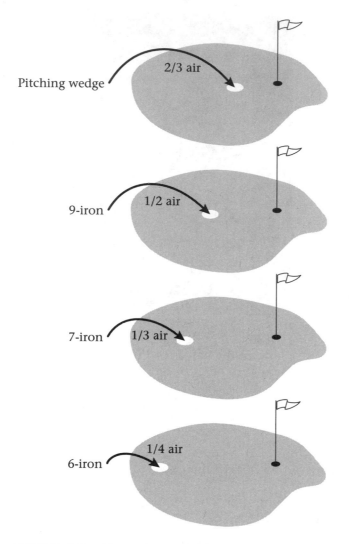

**FIGURE 5.3    Air to Ground Time for Chip Shot with Various Clubs and Landing Spots**

*1. Backswing.* The chip is a small swing motion that is completed with the arms and hands moving as one unit. Take your grip with the leading edge of the clubface square to an intermediate target. Move your arms, hands, and club back together (as with your putting stroke) while keeping your hands ahead of the clubface as illustrated in Figure 5.4.

**FIGURE 5.4  Backswing Front View**          **FIGURE 5.5  Impact**

*2. Downswing and Impact.*   The lower body is kept fairly still as you bring the club, hands, and arms back to the address position to contact the ball. The arms, hands, and club return to the ball as a unit, with the hands and butt end of the club still ahead of the clubface (Figure 5.5). Keep focused on the ball.

*3. Follow-Through.*   Keep the grip end moving toward the target. The distance of the follow-through should be as long as the backswing. On short chip shots, the follow-through should be low to the ground (Figure 5.6). Always remember to accelerate through the ball on all golf swings.

**FIGURE 5.6  Chipshot Follow-Through.** The triangle formed by the arms and hands remains throughout the chip swing motion. Right knee moves slightly toward the left knee on follow-through.

**Set-Up**

| | | |
|---|---|---|
| Grip | _____ | normal |
| Stance | _____ | narrow and open |
| Weight | _____ | toward target (left side) |
| Ball Position | _____ | center, or just rear of center, of stance and within 8 to 10 of toes |
| Clubface | _____ | square to intermediate target |
| Shoulders | _____ | square to target |
| Arms/hands | _____ | ahead of ball near left thigh |
| Knees/hips | _____ | flexed |

**Swing Mechanics**

| | | |
|---|---|---|
| Swing | _____ | one unit/single lever (like putting stroke) |
| Swing Arc | _____ | 7 to 8 o'clock—(backswing) with follow-through equal in length (5 to 4 o'clock) |
| Hands/arms | _____ | stay ahead of ball (short chips) |
| | _____ | move as one unit/wrists firm |
| | _____ | similar to putting stroke |
| | _____ | wrists hinge a little on longer shots |
| Swing Path | _____ | straight (short chips) like the putting stroke |
| Lower Body | _____ | movement reduced or still |

**FIGURE 5.7   Chipping Skill Builder Checklist**

---

**Chipping Skill Builders**

SET-UP DRILL

*Purpose:* Become familiar with the proper grip, stance, and posture for executing the chip shot. Figure 5.7 contains the Chipping Skill Builder Checklist.

*Equipment:* 7-, 8- or 9-iron, two yardsticks or two additional clubs

*Activity:*

1. Select a target. Let your partner place a target line on the ground with the first yardstick or club. Place an open stance line near the target line. Using the yardsticks as guides, set up to the ball. Try the set-up with the yardsticks five times in a row. Then switch with your partner. Repeat the procedure.
2. After your partner has had a turn, repeat the procedure but use an intermediate target without the yardsticks.
   Score = # of correct set-ups with no errors out of five trials: _____

SWING DRILL, NO BALL

*Purpose:* Become familiar with the correct swing movement and tempo.

*Equipment:* 7- or 8-iron

*Activity:*

1. Select a target and assume the correct grip, posture, and stance. Make a stroke as you would if you and were going to putt the ball.
2. Start out with short backswings and follow-throughs. Each should be the same length. Begin with a backswing just past your right foot and forward just past your left foot. Increase the swing distance each time but do not swing past your knee height.
3. Make ten swings with good tempo. Your partner should watch to see if: your wrists stay firm and the backswing and follow-through are of equal length; the club brushes the ground on each swing; your lower body remains fairly still; you focus on the ground until after the club brushes it.

## SWING DRILL WITH BALL

*Purpose:* Execute the chip swing motion with the ball and identify an acceptable landing area for the ball to reach the hole.

*Equipment:* 9-, 8-, and 7-iron, a rope about 5 feet long, two clubs or yardsticks

*Activity:*

1. Place the yardsticks parallel to each other with about 6 inches between them. Use them as guides for your swing path. Stand about 10 feet from the edge of the green.
2. The rope should be placed about 5 feet onto the green. The hole should be about 25 feet from the edge of the green.
3. Make a short swing, with just enough length to get the ball to land just over the rope. Hit ten balls each. Partners should assist each other with measuring how far the ball lands over the rope, determining correct set-up and swing length.

*Alternative Activity:*

4. Repeat the drill, moving the rope a little farther after identifying the correct landing area for each club to get the ball to the hole.
5. Repeat the drill without any props or guides.

Score = # of balls out of ten which land over the rope within 2 feet: _____

## CLUB ROTATION DRILL

*Purpose:* Experience the roll and trajectory of different lofted clubs while executing the chip shot.

*Equipment:* pitching wedge, 9-, 8-, and 7-irons, ten golf balls

*Activity:*

1. Begin chipping with the pitching wedge and note how far the ball travels, air time and ground time. Take an average out of five balls. Vary the swing length, making a longer swing, and record the distances.
2. Repeat the procedure with the pitching wedge, 9-, 8-, and 7-irons. Observe what happens in terms of the distance with the different clubs as you make the same swing length.

Score = # of correct club selections made from five locations around the green: _____

*Continued*

*Continued*

## CHIPPING TARGET DRILL

*Purpose:* To develop a feel for the swing length needed so the ball stops near the hole for a short putt of 2 to 3 feet.

*Equipment:* 8- or 7-iron, ten golf balls

*Activity:*

1. Set up to execute the shot. Take a practice swing or two of the length you think it will take to get the ball to stop near your target.
2. Execute the shot. Observe where the ball stops. If it stops short of the hole, lengthen your backswing. If it stops 3 to 5 feet past the hole, shorten the swing. If it stops to the left of the hole, aim a little more right of the hole and vice-versa. Be sure to use the same alignment procedures as you would for the full-swing set-up, selecting an intermediate target.
3. Strive to get the ball to stop within 1 to 3 feet of the hole so that you will have a short putt left to make.
4. Record your shot results: How many landed short of the hole? How many landed past? To the right or left? How many stopped within an acceptable area allowing a short putt?

Score = # of balls out of ten that stop within 3 feet or less of the hole at any point: _____

*Alternative Activity:*

1. Have a contest with a partner to see who can get the most chips to stop within 3 feet or less of the hole. Each person chips and whoever stops closest to the hole gets a point. See who can get to ten points first.
2. Change the distance from the green, moving back from the green.

## COMMON CHIPPING ERRORS AND CORRECTIONS

*Error:* Ball lands consistently off target.

*Correction:* Check alignment of the clubface and your body. Swing the club straight back and through, as with the putting stroke.

*Error:* Ball has a lot of air time and lands too short of the target.

*Correction:* Select a club with less loft. Too many golfers try to chip with a pitching wedge when there might be 30 feet of green to the pin. Try an 8- or 7-iron that will allow the ball to roll.

*Error:* Tries to lift the ball (scooping) with the hands, causing the clubhead to pass the hands. The result of this attempt is hitting behind the ball or sending it across the green.

*Correction:* The hands should be ahead of the ball during the set-up. Have someone check your set-up. Place the ball in the center in your stance. Make a descending blow to the ball. Practice the correct swing mechanics.

*Error:* Hits on top of the ball or misses it.

*Correction:* Keep wrists firm and arms straight throughout the swing. Keep posture the same throughout the swing. Your weight stays on the left or target side.

*Error:* Makes poor contact with the ball.

*Correction:* Keep the knees slightly flexed throughout the swing. The ball should be in back of or at the center of your stance and not forward. Keep your weight more on the left foot. The arms should hang straight down from your shoulders rather than reaching for the ball because of standing too far from the ball.

# 6

# PITCH SHOT

The pitch shot is played when the golfer needs a shot with a high trajectory followed by little roll. The idea is to get the ball in the air, and when it lands, having it stop fairly quickly for the regular pitch shot. The conditions in which the golfer would choose the pitch shot over the chip shot include the following: (1) a bunker or water lies between the player's ball position and the green (Figure 6.1);

**FIGURE 6.1   Pitch Shot.** Bunker lies between ball and green.

(2) a significant amount of grass is between the ball's position and the green, or the ball lies in the rough with too much grass to allow a chip shot; (3) the cup is near the fringe, and there is little green with which to work (Figure 6.2); and (4) the green's slope is steep and the ball needs to land softly and stop quickly. As a golfer just learning the game, you may find your approach shots to the green falling short. The pitch shot will aid you in getting the ball onto the green.

The clubs used to execute the pitch shot include the pitching wedge (PW), sand wedge (SW) or 9-iron. The pitching wedge is the club most often selected to make a pitch shot. However, many prefer to use a sand wedge or a specialty wedge with 60 degrees loft.

Beginning golfers may want to become somewhat skilled with a pitching wedge first, because there will be less chance of bouncing the club and skulling the ball using a sand wedge with a large flange on the sole of the club.

### Learner Skills

1. Explain the circumstances in which the pitch shot would be used over other types of shots.
2. Give a verbal description of the pitch shot.
3. Set up and demonstrate a mechanically sound pitch shot.

**FIGURE 6.2   Situation Requiring a Pitch Shot**

### Prerequisite Skills

1. Understands the concepts of grip, stance, ball position, weight distribution, posture, and alignment.
2. Understands the concepts of loft, trajectory, backswing, downswing, and follow-through.
3. Understands the difference between one-quarter, one-half, three-quarter swing length and the full swing.

## PITCH SHOT FUNDAMENTALS

### Address/Set-Up

**Stance.**   The feet should be placed inside the width of the shoulders but wider than the stance for the chip shot, although some players prefer a narrow stance on very short pitch shots. The stance should be slightly open on short pitch shots of up to 30 or 40 yards. The stance is only slightly open to square on longer pitch shots of 50 to 80 yards (Figure 6.3).

**FIGURE 6.3   Set-Up Pitch Shot.** Stance width is narrower than shoulders. Use normal grip. Keep ball near the center of the stance.

**Posture.**   Bend slightly forward at the hips, back straight, knees flexed a little. Your arms should hang in a relaxed manner vertically from your shoulders. The hands are just forward of the ball. Your shoulders need to be parallel to the target line (Figure 6.3).

**Ball Position.**   The ball should be placed at the center of the stance. If you want the ball to land softer and be more elevated, move the ball just forward of the center of your stance.

**Weight Distribution.**   Your weight should be evenly distributed between both feet on longer shots or a little more on the left (target) side for short pitch shots.

**Club Position.**   The clubface should be square to the target line.

**Grip.**   The grip is essentially the same as that for the full swing. When making short pitch shots, slide your hands about 3 or 4 inches toward the lower end of the grip. For longer pitch shots, the full length of the club should be used.

## Execution

**Backswing.**   The club is taken back with the arms and hands with some rotation of the shoulders in a single unit take-away as you would on the full swing (Figures 6.4 and 6.5).

Figure 6.5 shows that the wrists hinge just as the club passes waist height. Only a half-swing length is taken in this situation. The backswing is dictated by the distance the ball must travel. Notice at the top of the half backswing, the shoulders have turned about 60 to 70 degrees from their initial parallel position. The left arm points to about the 9 o'clock position. The lower body is quiet without much movement when executing the short pitch shot. The body's weight has shifted to the inside of the right foot, while the left heel still remains planted on the ground.

**Downswing.**   The downswing is initiated by pulling the club with the left arm on the inside of the target line. At the same time, the weight changes back toward the left foot as the clubhead descends toward the ball into the hitting zone (Figure 6.6).

**Impact.**   Avoid trying to scoop the ball with the right hand to get it airborne. The loft and weight of the club are designed to get the ball into the air. All you have to do is make a smooth, rhythmical swing. The same position you assumed at address should be duplicated as the ball is contacted with the arms fully extended to just past impact (Figure 6.7).

**FIGURE 6.4** Take-Away—
Initial Backswing

**FIGURE 6.5** Top of
Backswing—Short Pitch. Club
is moved more with shoulders,
arms, and hands, and the lower
body is less involved, as in the
full swing. Shoulders turn 60 to
70 degrees. Hands are at 9
o'clock, with wrists hinged.
Weight is shifted to inside of
right foot.

**Forwardswing and Finish.**    The forwardswing begins just after the ball is
contacted. The swing continues past the ball with the weight shifting more to
the left foot and the body turning toward the target. The club path is from
square, at impact, to down the target line, and then inside and parallel to your
stance line. The length of the follow-through portion of the swing should be
at least the backswing's length or a little longer. A little longer is better for most
situations. This will allow the club to be accelerated through the ball (Figures
6.8 and 6.9).

On short pitch shots, the club will need to go only waist high. In this case,
the club's toe will point more to a 2 o'clock position instead of straight up at

**FIGURE 6.6  Downswing.**
Wrists stay hinged until just
before impact.

**FIGURE 6.7  IMPACT!** Arms
are extended. Head remains
fairly still, with eyes focused
to where the ball is contacted.
Weight is on the left side.

**FIGURE 6.8A  Post-Impact
Forward Swing.** Head is still
focused on the impact spot.

**FIGURE 6.8B  Post-Impact
Follow-Through.** Top of club
points to sky at waist height.

**FIGURE 6.9    Finish.** The body is balanced over the left foot. The hands are at 2 o'clock—a bit higher than the backswing— which assures a good acceleration through the ball.

12 o'clock. Figures 6.8A and B illustrate the forwardswing. Figure 6.9 shows the finish. Notice the weight is on the left side, and the arms and hands have finished a little higher than the backswing length.

Figure 6.10 provides a Pitching Skill Builder Checklist for the pitch shot.

### Short Pitch Shot from the Rough

When the ball lies in the rough with a lot of grass between the ball and the green, a pitch shot is needed (Figure 6.11). In the rough, a sand wedge or pitching wedge is needed on a short shot. The shot is basically the same as a regular pitch shot. Here the stance is opened somewhat and the ball placed just a little back of center so a descending blow is made. On short shots like this one, the lower body is not as involved as in a longer shot. The shoulders, arms, and hands are used to take the club back.

**Set-Up**

Grip           ____ same as full swing/normal
                       ____ short pitch shot, grip down on the club a few inches

Stance        ____ narrower than shoulders
                       ____ open on short pitch shots
                       ____ square on longer pitch shots
                       ____ weight evenly distributed for long pitch
                       ____ weight more on the left side for short pitch shots

Shoulders/hips   ____ square to target line

Ball position     ____ center of stance

**Swing Mechanics**

Backswing    ____ 1/2 to 3/4 length to full (distance dictates swing length)

Wrists        ____ hinge at waist high (backswing for short pitch)
                       ____ hinge at waist high (target side for short pitch)
                       ____ full swing motion for long pitch

Weight shift    ____ shifts to inside of rear foot on backswing (right foot)
                       ____ short pitch—weight is set a little more on the left side

**Impact and Forwardswing**

Weight       ____ weight transfers to target foot (left foot) at impact and forwardswing

Arms         ____ extended at ball contact and at waist high on target side

**Finish/Follow through**

Finish         ____ right shoulder rotates under chin
                       ____ Head turns toward target
                       ____ arms extend to waist or shoulder high to complete the shot
                       ____ on short shots, clubface points at 2 o'clock at waist high instead of toe to the sky at 12 o'clock in the full swing

**FIGURE 6.10** **Pitching Skill Builder Checklist**

**FIGURE 6.11** **Pitch Shot from Rough Set-Up**

## Pitching Skill Builders

SET-UP DRILL

*Purpose:* Learn the correct set-up for the standard pitch shot.

*Equipment:* pitching wedge, or sand wedge, or 9–iron, ball, two yardsticks or additional clubs

*Activity:*

1. With the Pitching Skill Builder Checklist, you and your partner should go over the proper set-up components for the pitch as you assume each one. Your partner should make any corrections both verbally and physically if you need them.
2. Repeat the set-up with your partner only giving verbal cues.
3. Repeat the set-up with no cues from your partner.
4. Exchange places with your partner and repeat the procedure.

Score = # of set-ups made out of ten with no errors: _____

THUMBS-UP DRILL

*Purpose:* Feel the arm swing and wrist hinge during the pitch shot.

*Equipment:* none; for alternative activity, use a pitching wedge or 9-iron

*Activity:*

1. Set up with your arms hanging loose, palms together, as if gripping a club. Make a slow backswing with your hands to a 9 o'clock position. When you reach this clock position, hinge your wrists so that your thumbs point to the sky. Swing slowly forward as if to impact an imaginary ball and continue the swing to the 3 o'clock position on the opposite side. As you reach this clock position, the wrists should hinge again with thumbs pointing upward. Continue until the finish with your hands above your shoulders.
2. Repeat this procedure until you can make ten smooth swings with the correct wrist hinge. Your partner should check for the wrist hinge each time at both the backswing and follow-through positions. Switch and watch your partner complete the procedure.
3. You may repeat the drill with a tee placed in the hole of the butt end of a club. Watch the tee to see that it points to the ground on each backswing and at waist high on the forwardswing.

Score = # of correct backswing and follow-through positions out of ten trials: _____

PITCH WITH BALL

*Purpose:* Feel the swing motion with a ball.

*Equipment:* pitching wedge, sand wedge, or 9-iron; surveyor's flags or cones to indicate 20-, 30-, and 40-yard distances from the hitting area

*Activity:* Go to the first target. Set up correctly. Make a swing of half length. Check to be sure that a wrist hinge occurs at the backswing and follow-through. Note how far the ball travels in the air on each hit. Repeat the procedure at each distance.

*Alternative Activity:* Change clubs, making the same swing length (one-half) using the 9-iron and sand wedge. Note the difference in air distance with the 9-iron as compared to the pitching wedge and the sand wedge.

Score = air distance with each club for an average of ten balls:

PW _____    SW _____    9-iron _____

## VARIABLE SWING LENGTH DRILL

*Purpose:* To identify the distances the ball travels with different swing lengths with different clubs.

*Equipment:* pitching wedge, 9-iron, sand wedge, ten golf balls

*Activity:*

1. Start with a one-quarter swing length and hit ten balls. Record the average distance the ball actually travels with the club you are using. Continue the procedure with a one-half, three-quarter, and full swing. Using the hands at these clock positions, one-quarter length backswing = 8 o'clock; one-half length = 9 o'clock; three-quarter length = 10 o'-clock; full length = 11 o'clock.

2. Repeat the procedure until you have recorded the average distance the ball travels with all three clubs and swing lengths. Record the distance in yards that the ball travels based on your swing length:

|        | 1/4    | 1/2    | 3/4    | Full   |
|--------|--------|--------|--------|--------|
| SW     | _____ | _____ | _____ | _____ |
| PW     | _____ | _____ | _____ | _____ |
| 9-iron | _____ | _____ | _____ | _____ |

## ACCURACY DRILL

*Purpose:* To become proficient at getting the ball to stop near a target or hole on the green.

*Equipment:* green with holes, hitting distances marked at 20, 30, 40, and 50 yards from each hole; if no green is available, use a cone or mark a circle on the ground at 30-, 40-, and 50-yard distances from the hitting line

*Activity:*

1. Set up to the ball. Begin hitting to the 20-, 30-yard, then 40-yard and 50-yard distances, noting each time the variation in swing length needed to reach the target. Try to get the ball to stop within 5 to 10 yards of the target. Practice with ten balls at each distance. Then record the number of balls that stop within 5 to 10 yards of the target on either side of the hole.

   Club = _____

   30 yards _____/10    40 yards _____/10    50 yards _____/10

*Alternative Activity:*

2. From about 20 yards from the hole on the green, you and your partner pitch the ball onto the green. See how many putts it takes to hole the ball. The first one in the hole wins.

*Continued*

*Continued*

## COMMON PITCHING ERRORS AND CORRECTIONS

*Error:* Trajectory of the ball flight is low.

*Correction:* Check and be sure wrists hinge on backswing. Be sure the ball position is near the center of your stance; it may be too far forward.

*Error:* The ball is hit thin or topped.

*Correction:* Have your partner check your posture. You may be standing too upright for the length of the club. Keep proper body posture throughout the swing. Let your weight shift to your left foot on the forwardswing and follow-through. Avoid scooping at the ball with your hands; let the club's loft get the ball into the air. Keep your hands ahead of the clubhead, letting the clubhead descend to contact the ball.

*Error:* Contact with the ball is made with the hosel of the club.

*Correction:* You may be taking the club too far to the inside on the backswing, then trying to compensate on the downswing by moving first with the shoulders, thus getting the club closer to the ball by swinging out and down. You may be dipping your left shoulder down instead of making a good turn on the backswing.

*Error:* Hits are made on the ground behind the ball (fat shot).

*Correction:* Avoid lateral movement of the lower body. Be sure the ball is placed at the center of your stance. Check and be sure your hands are not too far ahead of the ball. Transfer your weight to the left side.

*Error:* Decelerates the club as it approaches the ball, finishing with a short follow-through.

*Correction:* The distance the ball needs to travel airborne dictates how far back to take the club on the backswing. A short pitch of 20 yards may only require a one-quarter backswing with as much or a little more follow-through. Avoid taking too long a backswing for the distance the ball must travel, which forces you to slow down as you approach the ball. Try the Variable Swing Length Drill.

# 7

# SPECIAL CIRCUMSTANCES

Golf courses are designed to be a challenge. This is one of the aspects of golf that makes the game exciting. Every shot you encounter will not always be from a nicely manicured fairway. Special circumstances include: (1) uneven lies; (2) play from the rough; (3) play from bunkers; (4) play from woods, pine needles, and loose dirt. However, knowing how to execute shots under these special circumstances, and keeping a cool head, will help you escape without the costly addition of too many strokes. These shots are not that difficult if you know how to modify the set-up and swing to match the conditions.

## Learner Skills

1. Explain the special circumstances under which the basic set-up for executing shots is modified
2. Demonstrate the set-up for bunker shots, uneven lies, and play from the rough and dirt.
3. Complete shots from a bunker with the ball landing outside the bunker.
4. Demonstrate club selection for different circumstances.
5. Execute shots, making solid contact with the ball placed in the rough.
6. Execute shots, making solid contact with the ball placed in an uneven lie—uphill, downhill, or sidehill.

## Prerequisite Skills

1. Understands alignment and can demonstrate a proper set-up needed to execute a full swing.
2. Understands the design of the golf club and what each club is designed to do.
3. Understands the typical layout of a golf hole.

## *UNEVEN LIES*

One of the most frequently encountered situations during a round of play is an uneven lie. This is when your ball comes to rest on a gentle to severe slope. As a result, your stance will not be flat—one foot will be higher than the other (up or downhill lies). or the ball may be higher or lower than your feet (sidehill lies).

In these situations, the four types of lies you may encounter are "sidehill," "uphill," and "downhill" lies, or combinations of these. A few simple adjustments need to be made to execute these shots. You might think of these situations as challenge shots or special circumstances rather than trouble.

### *Sidehill Lies*

Sidehill lies present circumstances in which the ball is either above or below your feet (Figures 7.1 and 7.2). These situations affect the flight of the ball. When the ball is higher than your feet, it tends to fly to the left for right-handers. Errors such as chunking, pulling, and hooking result. When the ball is

**FIGURE 7.1   Sidehill Lie.** Ball is above the feet. Aim to the right of the target, since the ball flies to the left in this situation.

**FIGURE 7.2   Sidehill Lie.** Ball is below feet. Aim left since ball will fly to the right.

below or lower than your feet, it tends to fly to the right. Errors include topping, pushing, and push-slicing. The steeper the slope, the more you must compensate for its directional effect. Remember that the ball follows the direction of the slope.

## Ball above the Feet

**Grip.**   If the slope is severe, gripping down on the club will be necessary. Before you set up to the ball, take a few practice swings to determine how far down to hold the club. In most cases, just a few inches will be necessary (Figure 7.1).

**Stance.**   When the slope is severe, your weight may need to be distributed more toward your toes to counteract balance against the slope, particularly when executing the swing. Assume your stance so the ball is positioned more toward the center. You will need to keep your body more upright, as the ball will naturally be closer to you.

**Club Selection.**   Because you will hold the club farther down the shaft, you may want a club with less loft. For instance, if you normally would use an 8-iron for the distance, you may select a 7-iron, as gripping down on the club decreases the distance it normally hits. You certainly do not want to swing harder with the 8-iron, because balance is more difficult to hold on a slope.

**Aim.**   Because the ball tends to hook or be pulled when it is above your feet, you will need to aim a little to the right of the target. How far depends on the severity of the slope and how the landing area slopes.

**Execution.**   Remember to visualize the shot and make the practice swing required for the distance the ball must travel. Then make a swing with good tempo and allow the club to do the work.

## Ball Below the Feet

The ball is actually lower than level ground, so there is a tendency to top the shot. Another problem is hitting the ball on the heel of the club, resulting in a shanked shot (the ball moves laterally to the right).

**Grip.**   Keep the grip in the normal position, as when executing a shot from flat lies. On steep slopes, you may need to grip the club as far toward the end as you can without jeopardizing your grip.

**Stance.**   Lean back toward your heels to maintain balance. You will need a little more flex in your knees on severe slopes. The flex needs to be maintained throughout your swing to avoid a topped or missed shot. You may want to widen your stance a little more for stability. Stand closer to the ball so it can be reached.

**Aim.**    Adjust your alignment more to the left of the target, as the ball will fly to the right (Figure 7.3).

**Execution.**    Again, visualize the shot, take one or two practice swings, then make a normal swing with good tempo.

## Downhill Lie

This shot presents a need for adjustment because the ball is below the level of your normal stance (Figure 7.4). The shot will generally fly to the right as a result of a push, fade, or slice. The clubface will be delofted when setting up to the ball in a downhill lie. This means that the ball will fly lower and longer. You may back up one club length, meaning that if you would normally use a 7-iron at this distance, select an 8-iron. Another option is to take less than a full swing to counteract the reduced loft on the selected club. A common error is to top the shot or hit the ball above its equator (thin shot).

**FIGURE 7.3    Ball Below the Feet.** This may require more flex in the knees and hips. Aim left of target when ball is below feet.

**FIGURE 7.4    Downhill Lie Set-Up.** Ball is placed near the high foot.

**Grip.** Make two practice swings to get the club contacting the ground in the correct spot. This will be slightly back of the center of your stance. Adjust your grip if necessary after the practice swings.

**Stance.** Set up so your stance is parallel to the slope. Lean your lower body into the slope to prevent gravity from pulling you off balance. Your shoulders should be parallel to the slope. Stand so the ball is near the high foot or slightly back of center.

**Aim.** Alignment needs to be adjusted to the left, as the ball tends to fade, be pushed, or sliced. Find an intermediate target that will align the clubface a few yards to the left of the target.

**Execution.** Take a normal swing at the ball. All the modifications in the set-up should allow the ball to land near your target if the swing was executed properly. Relax when executing the swing.

## Uphill Lie

In this situation, the ball has a tendency to fly left, or result in a pulled shot, or even a pull-hook if the clubface is closed. It is also difficult to make a good weight transfer with an uphill lie, as gravity is pulling you back from the intended target. A common mistake is to use less club than is necessary, because the slope tends to add loft to the club, which causes the ball to fly higher and not as far as it normally would with a flat lie. There are some modifications that need to be made to execute a shot in this situation (Figure 7.5).

**Grip.** Grip down on the club a few inches. You will need one or two clubs longer than normal (less loft). If you are at a distance in which you would normally use a sand wedge, you might select a 9- or even an 8-iron.

**Stance.** You must resist the pull of gravity, so you will need to lean more to the left. Your shoulders must be parallel to the slope. Place the ball just ahead of center or toward the higher foot (left foot) (Figure 7.6).

**Aim.** Align to the right of the target, as the ball tends to fly to the left.

**Execution.** Take one or two practice swings to get a feel for the shot. Check to see that you have gripped down enough on the club. This will help you to determine if you are set up correctly. If you are not set up correctly, most likely you will jab the club into the ground, hitting behind the ball. Remember, the swing must follow the slope.

Figure 7.7 depicts the Uneven Lies Skill Builder Checklist. The type of slope is indicated, the effects, and the adjustments necessary to execute the shot.

**FIGURE 7.5    Uphill Lie.** Ball is placed forward of center or near the higher foot on the slope.

**FIGURE 7.6    Uphill Lie.** Ball tends to fly to the left. Aim a little to the right.

**Uneven Lies Skill Builders**

BALL ABOVE AND BELOW THE FEET DRILL (SET-UP)

*Purpose:* To assume the correct set-up for executing the shot.

*Equipment:* two yardsticks, one copy of Uneven Lies Skill Builder Checklist, 7-, 8-, or 9-iron.

*Activity:*

1.  One partner will practice while the other checks the adjustments needed to execute the shot. The hitter will align for an uphill lie. Line up one yardstick on the target (target line). With an uphill lie, you need to align to the right of the target. Place the other yardstick to the right of the original target line. Align your feet and shoulders parallel to this line and the clubface square to this line. Your partner should give you a verbal cue for each modification.
2.  Repeat the set-up sequence without verbal cues from your partner, unless you need them. Repeat the set-up until you can complete it correctly without verbal cues.
3.  Partners exchange places and repeat the procedure.
4.  Repeat the activity with the ball below your feet.

Score = # of times out of ten you can set up without errors: _____

**Ball Below Feet**

Slope Effect
- Ball flies right

Modification
_____ aim to the left
_____ flex knees more with weight more on heels
_____ grip near the end
_____ keep knees flexed throughout swing
_____ ball placed near center of stance

**Ball Above Feet**

Slope Effect
- Ball flies left

Modification
_____ aim to the right
_____ grip down 1 or 2 inches, depending on the steepness of the slope
_____ weight should be more on the balls of the feet
_____ ball should be near the center of stance

**Uphill Lie**

Slope Effect
- Ball is pulled to the left
- Ball flies shorter and higher

Modification
_____ grip down on the grip
_____ lean lower body into the hill
_____ shoulders parallel to slope
_____ position ball forward of center or nearer the high foot
_____ select a club with less loft, i.e., 9-iron instead of pitching wedge.

**Downhill Lie**

Slope Effect
- Shot is pushed right

Modification
_____ lean into the hill with the weight on your right foot
_____ shoulders must be parallel to the slope
_____ ball is placed back of center or toward the high foot
_____ aim to the left of your intended target

Total Score = 1 point for each subskill, 19 points possible: _____  _____

                                                                      pre test       post test

**FIGURE 7.7 Uneven Lies Skill Builder Checklist**

BALL ABOVE AND BELOW THE FEET-SWING FEEL

*Purpose:* Develop a feel for the swing and make swings with balance and tempo.

*Equipment:* 6- or 7-irons.

*Activity:*
1. Work with a partner. One person should set up correctly to the ball above the feet. Your partner should check for the correct set-up position using the Skill Builder Checklist for Uneven Lies. Swing the club with a relaxed swing motion. The club needs to follow the slope. Continue to make swings, striving for a smooth swing with good tempo. Concentrate on maintaining balance throughout the swing. Let your partner repeat the activity.

Score = # of swings out of ten made with tempo and balance: _____

*Continued*

*Continued*

2. Repeat this activity with a ball below the feet lie.

Score = # of swings out of ten made with tempo and balance: _____

## BALL ABOVE AND BELOW THE FEET—CHIP AND PITCH DRILL

*Purpose:* To develop skill in chipping and pitching from a below and above the feet lie.

*Equipment:* pitching wedge, 9-iron, circle marked with flags, ten golf balls

*Activity:* Practice each shot with the ball placed above your feet and below your feet. Initially concentrate on making solid contact with the ball. Try to get the balls to stop within 3 to 5 feet of the target for chipping and 5 to 10 feet of the target for pitching. The target should be about 30 to 40 feet away for chipping and 20 to 30 yards for pitching.

Goal = # of balls out of ten stopping within 3 feet of the target for chipping: _____

Goal = # of balls out of ten stopping within 5 feet of the target for pitching: _____

## UPHILL AND DOWNHILL LIES

Repeat the same activities for sidehill lies.
    *Note:* If no slope is available, place one foot on the edge of a golf bag, small bucket, or auto tire to get the feel of one foot being higher than the other.

Goal = # of balls out of ten hit with solid contact (downhill): _____

Goal = # of balls out of ten hit with solid contact (uphill): _____

## ERRORS AND CORRECTIONS

### Sidehill Lies—Ball Above Feet

*Error:* Hits the ground before the ball—a fat shot.

*Correction:* Grip down on the club and take practice swings to get the feel for the shot. The ball should be positioned near the center of your stance. Make sure your weight shifts back to the left on the downswing.

*Error:* The ball travels left of the intended target.

*Correction:* Compensate by aiming to the right of the intended target, as the ball tends to hook or be pulled with this lie. Be sure to align parallel to the intermediate target to the right.

*Error:* The ball does not go as far as it needs to go.

*Correction:* Select one club less than you would normally use for the distance needed.

*Error:* Balance is frequently lost while executing this shot.

*Correction:* Counteract the pull of gravity. Stand with your weight more on the balls of your feet. Take one club less than needed for the distance and make a good smooth swing with balance and tempo.

### Ball Below Feet

*Error:* Ball contact is made with the heel of the club—shanked.

*Correction:* Flex your knees more than in a normal stance and stay flexed throughout the swing. Keep weight on your heels; do not fall forward on your toes. Stand a little closer to the ball to avoid reaching for it and contacting the ball with the heel of the club.

*Error:* Ball is topped.

*Correction:* Stay in the flexed-knee posture throughout the swing. Take practice swings to be sure the swing contacts the ground. Ball should be positioned near the center of your stance. Grip the club near the butt end of the grip; do not choke down.

*Error:* Ball misses target to the right.

*Correction:* The ball tends to fly in this direction from this lie. Select an intermediate target to the left and align parallel to it.

### Downhill Lie

*Error:* The ball is topped, whiffed, or club hits ground behind the ball.

*Correction:* Ball should be positioned back of center or nearer the high foot on the slope. Shoulders must be parallel to or match the slope. Maintain posture throughout the swing, especially leg and hip flex.

*Error:* The ball travels farther when hit with the same club from a flat lie.

*Correction:* This lie tends to deloft the club, so select one club more: If a 7-iron is used for the distance from a flat lie, use an 8- or 9-iron, depending on the steepness of the slope.

### Uphill Lie

*Error:* Shots are pulled or they end up left of the intended target.

*Correction:* This lie causes the ball to be pulled. Select an intermediate target to the right of the intended target and align parallel to the intermediate target.

*Error:* The ball does not travel as far when hit with the same club from a flat lie.

*Correction:* This lie tends to add loft to the club because of the slope. Select one club less: Use an 8- or 9-iron where you would normally select a pitching wedge.

*Error:* The club is jabbed into the turf rather than contacting the ball and following the slope.

*Correction:* Match your shoulders to the up slope or make them parallel to the slope. Place the ball just forward of center or nearer the high foot on the slope. Take practice swings to gauge the movement of the club along the slope.

## PLAY FROM THE ROUGH

The rough is the unmowed, high-grass area on either side of the fairway or near the green. If your tee or fairway shot should stray toward the rough, the first thing to do is watch it very carefully and spot a landmark at the point where it entered the rough. The first step to exiting this situation is that you have to be able to find your ball.

The rough can be short and your ball may have a good lie, which does not present too much of a challenge. On the other hand, the ball may be in tall rough with a bad lie. Now you have a challenge but not an impossible shot with a few adjustments made to account for a lie in deep rough.

### Steps for Playing from the Rough

1. When you find a ball, check it to be sure it is your ball. If you hit the wrong ball, it is a two-stroke penalty.
2. Determine if the ball is playable or declare an unplayable lie.
3. Determine the condition of the rough; Is it short rough and the ball has a good or somewhat good lie? Or is it deep rough?
4. Determine a target. Ask yourself these questions: How much rough lies between you and the fairway or green? What is a realistic target? What is the best club to use? Your only option may be your sand wedge. If you are 130 yards from the green, you cannot try to reach it from this situation.

Remember, the goal is to recover from this situation so that you will have a relatively easy shot from the fairway or a short shot to land on the green. You could use the wrong club or go for the long shot and end up with one, two or even three more strokes added to your score because you did not exit the rough with the shot. In deep rough, you could easily lose the ball by trying heroic shots.

### Procedures for Short Rough

In some cases, you might end up in short rough. The grass may be slightly longer than the fairway, but the ball has a good or semi-good lie. The following steps will lead to a good shot from this situation. You may be 100 yards from your target, which could be the green. Select the club you usually hit 90 to 100 yards. Figure 7.8 depicts the set-up from short rough.

**Grip.**   Use a normal grip.

**Stance.**   Your stance width is normal, but weight should be a little more on the left side. The ball should be a little back in your stance.

**Posture.**   The hands should be more in front of the ball than in the normal set-up routine.

**Execution.**   Take a normal swing with tempo and balance.

**FIGURE 7.8   Set-Up—Short Rough**

## Procedures for Less than Good Lie in Rough

A successful execution from the rough where the ball may have less than a good lie depends on a good plan. Determine the lie of the ball. The grass will reduce the club speed. Also, grass behind the ball will affect the clubface at impact, closing it. This will result in a ball flying left, low, and longer than usual. Select a club with more loft to compensate for the lower and longer flight. If the distance permits, use a 7- or 8-iron instead of a 6-iron.

If the ball is sitting up in the rough, be careful not to move it when setting up and taking a practice swing. If you move the ball, it is a one-stroke penalty. Take your practice swing away from the ball. You must select a reachable and realistic target. Going for the green may be a big mistake and add strokes to your score. Figure 7.9 illustrates the set-up for executing shots with less than good lies from the rough.

**Grip.**   Use a normal grip but open the clubface, first, a little; grip down some for control.

**Stance.**   Widen your stance somewhat. The ball should be positioned back in your stance or right of center. Distribute your weight more on the left side.

**Execution.**   Take a normal smooth swing.

**FIGURE 7.9   Set-Up for Poor
Lies from the Rough**

### Procedures for Thick Rough

Sometimes your ball will end up in thick rough and have a bad lie. This is not the time to try heroic shots. All you want to do is get the ball back to the fairway so your next shot will be easy to execute.

### Procedures

Select a sand wedge if you have one or open the face on a pitching wedge. You can always opt for an unplayable lie, take a penalty stroke, and drop the ball behind a line on your ball and the hole.

Sometimes a fairway wood, such as a 5- or 7-wood, will work in rough, as the sole is rounded and will slide through the grass. Again, the distance will have an impact on club selection.

**Grip.**   Grip farther down and hold a little firmer than normal but not tightly. Open the clubface before gripping.

**Stance.**   The ball needs to be in back of the stance, near the right foot. Widen your stance more than you would when playing the wedge from a normal lie. Distribute your weight more on the left foot. Open your stance.

**Posture.**   Your hands should be ahead of the ball.

**Execution.**   Aim a little left of your target to allow for an open stance and clubface. Visualize the shot. The set-up helps you to make a steep or "V"-shaped backswing, which is necessary to avoid catching the club in the grass and making a descending blow to the ball.

Make a smooth backswing, bending the wrists, creating a sharp upswing. The downswing descends sharply to and under the ball. Follow through to the finish. You must make a descending blow to the ball and follow through. The lower body stays fairly quiet with some weight shift on the downswing and follow-through. This shot is executed more with the upper body, as if playing a sand shot.

Figure 7.10 includes a Skill Builder Checklist for play from the rough. Shots from short and thick rough are included with good and bad lies.

---

**Short Rough—Good Lie**

*Grip*

_____   grip down about 2 inches for control

*Ball Position*

_____   center

*Club Selection*

_____   lofted wood, 5 or 7

_____   same club you would hit in the fairway

*Execution*

_____   normal swing

**High Rough**

*Grip*

_____   open clubface, then grip down

*Stance*

_____   open

_____   weight more on left foot

_____   ball positioned just rear of center

*Club Selection*

_____   sand or pitching wedge

*Execution*

_____   aim left of target

_____   swing along body line, making a descending blow

**Short Rough—Bad Lie**

*Grip*

_____   open clubface, then grip down

*Ball Position*

_____   slightly right or back of center

*Stance*

_____   open slightly

_____   weight more on the left foot

*Club Selection*

_____   no less than a 6- or 7-iron

*Execution*

_____   aim a little left of the target swing upright on backswing

_____   make a descending blow on downswing

*Comments:*

---

**FIGURE 7.10   Play from the Rough Skill Builder Checklist**

**Play from the Rough Skill Builders**

SET-UP DRILL—GOOD LIE IN SHORT ROUGH

*Purpose:* To develop a correct set-up for shots from the rough with a good lie.

*Equipment:* 7-, 8-, or 9-iron, golf ball

*Activity:*

1. One partner reviews the Rough Skill Builder Checklist out loud as the other partner sets up to hit the ball. Set up again, without verbal cues from your partner, unless you request them. Continue setting up until you can do so correctly five times in a row with no errors.
2. Switch places with your partner and repeat the above procedures.

Score = # of correct set-ups with no errors out of ten trials: _____

SHORT ROUGH—BAD LIE

Repeat the procedures in the previous drill following the Rough Skill Builder Checklist procedures for short rough–bad lie.

Score = # of correct set-ups with no errors out of ten trials: _____

HIGH ROUGH

Repeat the procedures in the previous drill following the Rough Skill Builder Checklist procedures for high rough.

Score = # of correct set-ups with no errors out of ten trials: _____

PITCH SHOT FROM HIGH ROUGH

*Purpose:* Develop a feel for executing a pitch shot from high rough.

*Equipment:* sand wedge, ten golf balls, 20-foot-diameter circle in center of green or fairway

*Activity:*

1. Set up and execute the shot 20 yards from the circle. Weight should be more on the left side, with the lower body less active than in the normal swing. Make the shot with the upper body. Try to get the ball airborne and have it stop in the circle.
2. Allow your partner a turn after the balls have been retrieved. Continue taking turns until you have had at least three turns. Use the Rough Skill Builder Checklist to help your partner set up correctly each time.

Score = # of balls out of ten stopping in the circle: _____

ERRORS AND CORRECTIONS

*Bad Lie—Rough*

*Error:* Ball flies a very short distance with club catching in grass.

*Correction:* Select a lofted club—sand or pitching wedge. Open the clubface and grip down a little. Make an upright swing to make a descending blow to the ball. Follow through and finish the swing.

*Error:* Ball hooks.

*Correction:* Clubface tends to close when contacting the taller grass. Aim a little to the right of the target. Or open the clubface to counteract its closing as it contacts the grass.

## PLAY FROM BUNKERS

If you play golf, eventually you will land in a bunker with sand. One way to become skilled at exiting the bunker on the first try is to practice the shot. This sounds simple, but many golfers do not practice sand shots, and when they land in a bunker, however unintentionally, they do not have a plan for getting out of the situation. With some knowledge of how to adjust your set-up, how the sand wedge works, and how to swing, this shot is no big deal.

### Types of Bunkers

There are two types of bunkers on the golf course—fairway bunkers and greenside bunkers. Fairway bunkers are strategically placed to capture a tee shot or a fairway shot on a par 4 or 5. These may be on the left or right edges of the fairway. Greenside bunkers are placed around the greens.

Even the type of sand may vary from one course to another. Sand is brown and coarse in some bunkers, white and fine on other golf courses. And, when the weather changes, for example after a hard rain, the sand may become packed and hard, which presents a unique situation. In this case, a pitching wedge should be used instead of a sand wedge. It will be important for you to be able to "read" the sand as you would "read" a green before putting.

### Challenges Presented by Bunkers

Because you will be standing in sand most of the time to execute a shot from the bunker, your stance will be affected. There will not be as much stability as you would have when hitting from the grass.

Your choice of club will be the sand wedge most of the time in a greenside bunker. The sand wedge is designed a little differently from other clubs. Figure 7.11 illustrates the clubhead of sand wedges compared to other clubs such as the pitching wedge. The sand wedge is designed to hit a shot in sand and has a loft of 56 degrees or more. It may also be used to make shots from deep rough. The sole of the sand wedge is wider than the bottom of other clubs, and it rests lower than the leading edge of the clubface. This wide bottom of the sand wedge is referred to as the "flange." This is what gives the club's head bounce through the sand and prevents it from digging into the sand. Actually, as you swing the club, the flange acts like a grader and moves the sand forward, carrying the ball with it (Figure 7.12).

Think of the wedge as the power source that departs energy to the sand, which in turn transfers the energy to the ball and launches it. It is like splashing water in a pool. To splash someone, you cut into the water at a shallow angle, creating a wave of airborne water. This is what you do with the sand wedge to get the ball out of the sand. The sand acts as a wave. In fact, the shot from the bunker is sometimes called a "splash shot." The pitching wedge might be the choice for executing the shot when the ball has a buried lie, in which case you need a club to "dig" at the sand to move the ball.

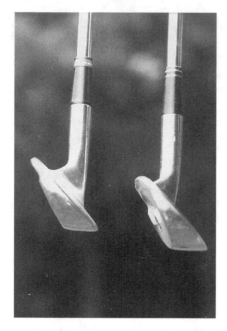

**FIGURE 7.11  Pitching Wedge and Sand Wedge.** Note the wide flange on sand wedge on the right.

**FIGURE 7.12  How the Sand Wedge Works.** Sand wedge pushes sand forward, giving the ball a ride.

## Good Lies and Buried Lies

The ball may stop in the bunker and rest nicely on top of the sand. This would be fortunate, as the ball would have a good lie. On the other hand, if you hit a high shot and the ball lands in soft sugary sand, it may create a crater. In this situation, the ball is not buried, but neither is it resting on top, so the lie will be half good. In some cases, the ball may be nearly buried in soft fluffy sand— a bad lie. Figure 7.13 illustrates a good lie, a half-buried lie, and a buried lie in the bunker.

## Escaping Safely

To get out of the bunker with as few strokes as possible is the idea. To get out of the bunker in one stroke is the goal. The following are basic steps to follow in any bunker situation.

**FIGURE 7.13   Lie of the Ball in the Sand Dictates Type of Shot.** Good lie, half-buried lie, buried lie.

**Step 1.**   Do not panic. Be calm and, most of all, confident that you can execute the shot.

**Step 2.**   Analyze the situation as you approach the bunker. Where is the ball—in the center, at the back, next to the lip of the bunker?

**Step 3.**   What kind of lie does the ball have? Is it a good lie, resting on top of the sand? Is it a half-good lie, only slightly or half buried? Is it buried or plugged? Is it a flat lie—uphill, downhill, or sidehill? Is the bunker shallow or steep?

**Step 4.**   The sand will generally be white and powdery, brown and coarse, loose or packed. What is the condition here? Is it packed and shallow, loose and grainy, powdery with fine texture and fluffy?

**Step 5.**   If you are in a greenside bunker, where is the pin placed on the green? Do you have a lot of green with which to work? Or is the pin placed close to the bunker, giving you very little green?

## Execution—Good Lie

The following procedures or steps will aid you in the proper set-up and execution from a greenside bunker situation when the ball has a good lie. Once you have analyzed the situation as depicted in the five steps above, you are ready to execute the sand shot.

**Grip.**    First, open the clubface on the sand wedge, then take a normal grip, gripping down a couple of inches to get better control of the club (Figure 7.14).

Do not grip the club then open the clubface. Take your grip before you enter the bunker. If you touch the sand with the club except on the downswing, it is a two-stroke penalty. Take practice swings outside the bunker.

**Stance.**    Open your stance aligning your feet, shoulders, and hips to the left of the target. Open your stance about as much as the clubface is open to the right. The width of your stance should be narrower than your shoulders. Dig your feet into the sand slightly to establish a firm stance. You do not have to dig in deep. Be sure you align the clubface to the desired target by moving your body to the left until the clubface is squared to the intermediate target. Figure

**FIGURE 7.14  Club Position for Sand Shot with a Good Lie.** Sand shot, good lie.

**FIGURE 7.15  Set Up for Good Lie in the Sand**

7.15 illustrates the set-up. Your weight should be distributed a little more to the left side. Position the ball just forward of the center of your stance.

**Posture.**    Flex your knees and let your arms hang loosely from your shoulders. Your hands should be just slightly in front of the ball.

**Backswing.**    The open stance will allow you to make an upright backswing. Make a smooth backswing, keeping your arms and hands relaxed, flexing your wrists early. Your swing follows your stance line to the left of the target (Figure 7.16).

### Downswing and Impact

- Arms and hands start the club downward as a single unit. The lower body is not as active as in a normal swing, but you will feel the weight shift to the left side.
- Focus on the sand more so than on the ball. You will contact the sand about 2 to 3 inches behind the ball (Figure 7.17). The energy imparted to the sand will lift the ball and carry it forward (Figure 7.18).

**FIGURE 7.16  Upright Backswing**

**FIGURE 7.17  Where to Contact the Sand.** Splash the sand just a couple of inches behind the ball.

**FIGURE 7.18   Downswing for Sand Shot.** Extend arms at impact. Contact sand a couple of inches behind the ball.

**FIGURE 7.19   Follow Through on Sand Shot.** You must follow through.

**Follow-Through.**   Accelerate through and finish the swing at least as high as the backswing, keeping the clubface open most of the way through the finish (Figure 7.19).

### Sand Shot—Half-Buried Lie

**Grip.**   Use a normal grip with the clubface square, gripping down about 2 inches on the shaft.

**Stance.**   Firm your stance by digging in slightly, not too deeply. Your stance should be narrower than your shoulders and square to an intermediate target, not open as when the ball has a good lie. Distribute your weight more on the left side (Figure 7.20).

**Ball Position.**   The ball needs to be one or two ball lengths back from the center of your stance to allow a steeper approach on the downswing.

**FIGURE 7.20  Set-Up for Half-Buried Lie**

**FIGURE 7.21  Backswing for Half-Buried Lie**

**Posture.**  Your hands should be placed just in front of the ball. Figure 7.20 illustrates the set-up for this shot.

**Execution.**

*Backswing.*  Hinge your wrists early to create a vertical backswing, still moving the arms and hands as a unit (Figure 7.21).

*Downswing and Impact.*  Descend the club downward, contacting the sand just a couple of inches behind the ball. Accelerate through keeping your hands ahead of the club.

*Forwardswing and Follow-Through.*  Continue to follow through and finish the swing. The ball will not land as softly as it does when there is a good lie. Because the clubface is square, and more sand impacts the ball, it flies farther and rolls farther. There is very little, if any, backspin on the ball.

## Plugged or Buried Lie

The ball sometimes gets buried in soft sand with only the top of it even with the sand. This usually results when the ball enters the bunker from a high trajectory. This shot is made similarly to the half-buried lie, with just a few adjustments. Figure 7.22 illustrates the set-up and swing sequence for the plugged lie. This shot has more roll than a regular shot from the sand. It does not stop quickly on the green.

**Grip.**   Square or close the clubface and then grip the club firmly about 2 or 3 inches down the shaft. Use a pitching wedge.

**Stance.**   Dig your feet into the sand, with your stance narrower than your shoulders and with your weight very much on the left side. The stance should be closed to the intermediate target.

**Ball Position.**   Place the ball well in back of your stance.

**FIGURE 7.22   Set-Up for Buried Lie**

**Posture.**   Your arms and hands need to be in front of the ball so your backswing will be upright, allowing you to make a stabbing, descending blow to the sand.

**Swing/Execution.**

*Backswing.*   Immediately hinge the wrists with arms and hands moving as a unit to the top. Be sure to make a good shoulder turn (Figure 7.23).

*Downswing.*   Pull the club down sharply, letting it contact the sand just behind the ball as if to drive a big nail into the ground. More sand will be moved and have a tendency to open the clubface, which is why it needs to be closed. Make every effort to accelerate through the ball, which will not be as easy in this situation (Figures 7.24A and 7.24B).

*Follow-Through.*   Try to follow through, which is harder to do in this case. Concentrate on the target (Figure 7.24C).

**FIGURE 7.23   Backswing for Buried Lie**

**FIGURE 7.24A**   Impact—
Buried Lie

**FIGURE 7.24B**   Forward
Swing—Buried Lie

**FIGURE 7.24C**   Follow
Through Is Important

**Sand Shot Skill Builders**

CLUBFACE ADJUSTMENT

*Purpose:* To experience adjusting the clubface to open and closed positions.

*Equipment:* pitching wedge and sand wedges

*Activity:*

1. Practice gripping the club as you normally do for standard shots.
2. Open the clubface about 45 degrees by holding it with your right hand. Grip down about 2 inches with your left hand, then with the right hand as if taking a normal grip.
3. Have your partner inspect your grip and check for the open clubface position. Repeat the procedure five times and let your partner repeat it.
4. Repeat the activity closing the clubface.

Score = # of grips taken correctly out of five trials, open: _____ ; closed: _____

SAND SET-UP WITH A GOOD LIE

*Purpose:* To become familiar with setting up to make a sand shot with a good lie.

*Equipment:* one sand wedge, Sand Shot Skill Builder Checklist, two yardsticks

*Activity:*

1. Stand in the bunker. Open the clubface and grip the club. Open your stance about as much as you have opened the clubface. Adjust your stance to the left of a target until the clubface is square to the target. Be sure you have not opened your stance too much. Use the yardsticks to mark the stance and target lines.
2. Swing the club along your stance line. Switch and let a partner have a turn.
3. Use the Sand Shot Skill Builder Checklist to assist.

Score = # of correct set-ups out of five trials: _____

MOVING SAND DRILL

*Purpose:* Develop feel for moving the sand with the club.

*Equipment:* sand wedge and at least one bunker with sand

*Activity:*

1. Draw a small circle about 4 inches in diameter in the sand. Set up as if a golf ball were resting in the middle of the circle. Use the Sand Shot Skill Builder Checklist to help you with the set-up.
2. Make a three-quarter swing, contacting the sand at the edge of the back of the circle. Accelerate through and finish the swing. The sand should move in the direction the clubface was aligned.
3. Make ten swings, trying to move the little circle of sand. Switch and let your partner try the activity.
4. Repeat the activity, except make a ridge of sand about 3 feet long and 1 inch high.

Score = # of circles moved out of ten: _____

*Continued*

*Continued*

## LINE-AND-BALL DRILL

*Purpose:* To contact the sand and carry the ball out of the bunker.

*Equipment:* golf balls, sand wedge, pitching wedge

*Activity:*

1. One partner sets up to hit a sand shot with a good lie, using a sand wedge. One partner reviews the set-up procedures using the Sand Shot Skill Builder Checklist. You may touch the sand during your set-up in this drill for practice purposes only.
2. Have your partner mark a line from the center of your stance to about 3 feet in front of you. Swing the club as if you were going to hit a sand shot and note where you contact the sand each time. Place a ball about 1 to 2 inches in front of that spot. Repeat the set-up and try to get the ball out by hitting the sand.
3. Exchange places with your partner and repeat the activity. Exchange places again and repeat the activity. This time, one partner can practice setting up outside the bunker for a buried lie sand shot, using the pitching wedge.

*Alternate Activity:* Repeat the procedures above setting up to hit a sand shot from a buried lie.

Score = # of shots hit out of the bunker out of ten trials: _____

## DISTANCE DRILL

*Purpose:* To learn to vary the distance the ball travels out of the bunker.

*Equipment:* sand wedges for each pair and 10 golf balls

*Activity:*

1. Have your partner review the set-up for a good lie. Take a half backswing and follow through, hitting balls out of the bunker. Note how far the balls travel. You may contact the sand during the set-up and backswing for practice purposes.
2. Adjust your swing length to hit balls near the 5-yard target. Let your partner try the activity.
3. Try to hit to the 10-yard target, noting how much to adjust your backswing.
4. Let your partner try the activity. Try to hit to the 15-yard target, noting how much you need to adjust your swing length. Let your partner try.

*Additional Activity:* After each partner begins to be successful, one calls out a target and the person hitting tries to get the ball within 10 feet of the target. Repeat, calling out different targets each time.

*Additional Activity:* Repeat the procedure, but set up and hit buried-lie shots.

Goal = # of good-lie shots out of six trials that land within 10 feet of
each target:     _____  _____     _____
                   5 yards    10 yards     15 yards

Goal = # of buried-lie shots out of six trials that land within 10 to 15 feet of
each target:     _____  _____     _____
                   5 yards    10 yards     15 yards

*Additional Activity:* Repeat all bunker drills *without* grounding the club in the bunker. Set up with the clubface just above the sand. Do not touch the sand during the backswing. If you touch the sand, USGA Rules state it is a two-stroke penalty in stroke play and loss of the hole in match play.

## COMMON ERRORS AND CORRECTIONS

*Error:* The ball rather than the sand is contacted.

*Correction:* Check to see if the ball is correctly aligned in your stance. For good lies, the ball should be just slightly in front of center. For half-good lies, or a ball slightly buried in sand, the ball should be one or two ball lengths to the rear of center. For buried lies, the ball should be in line with your right instep. Steepen and lengthen your backswing.

*Error:* You lose your balance or your feet slide around while executing your sand shot.

*Correction:* Dig your feet slightly down in the sand to prevent sliding.

*Error:* The club bounces into the ball rather than moving the sand first.

*Correction:* Be sure your hands are just slightly ahead of the ball when it has a good lie and farther ahead when the ball has a buried lie.

*Error:* The ball moves only a short distance, remaining in the bunker.

*Correction:* Be sure to accelerate through the sand to finish the swing. The follow-through will need to be as long as your backswing length. Transfer your weight fully onto your left foot.

## FAIRWAY BUNKER SHOTS

In most instances, a fairway club such as a 5- or 7-wood may be used to execute shots from fairway bunkers (Figure 7.25). Irons are also used to execute fairway bunker shots. The club selection depends on the lie of the ball and the distance to the green. If the bunker has a high lip, a club that will elevate the ball enough to get it over the lip will be necessary. A good lie with room to clear the low lip of a bunker would allow a shot with a wood, if the distance required it. A half-buried lie near the front of a bunker would require a 7-, 8-, or 9-iron.

## UNEVEN LIES IN BUNKERS

Sometimes, you may have an uphill or downhill lie in the bunker. In this case, the procedures used for uneven lies would be followed to execute the shot. Also, if the ball is above or below your feet, follow the same procedures as if you had this lie in the fairway.

Most sand shots will be from greenside bunkers. Figure 7.26 provides a Sand Shot Skill Builder Checklist. Procedures for a good lie are suggested, and modifications are indicated for half-buried and buried lies.

**FIGURE 7.25    Wood Shot from a Fairway Bunker (good lie)**

## PLAY FROM THE WOODS

Sometimes, a tee shot or fairway shot will end up in the woods. If the woods are not designated as out of bounds by white stakes, you have the option of hitting the ball with no penalty. The ground will obviously not be like the fairway. In fact, it will often have leaves, twigs, pine needles, rocks, or roots in the way of your swing. Follow these steps for getting safely out of the woods: Locate your ball and be sure it is yours; remain calm and study the situation—determine the lie, look for an exit route, note if you have a full swing or partial swing, examine the ground to see if there are loose impediments to interfere with your swing. Remember, the idea is to get the ball back in play so you will have a better shot situation.

You may move loose impediments such as twigs and stones, but be careful not to move the ball; otherwise a one-stroke penalty incurs. You may have to declare the lie unplayable, take a drop, take a stroke, and go on with the play. If you decide that the ball is playable, visualize the shot, select the club, practice the swing, set up, and execute the shot.

If the ground is hard or is covered with pine needles, loose sand, or dirt, play the ball back of center in your stance and use a club with some loft—a 7- or 8-iron. This will get the ball elevated and back into the fairway and reduce the chances of hitting the ground first.

|  | Good Lie | Half-Buried Lie | Buried Lie |
|---|---|---|---|
| Grip | ___ open clubface | ___ square | ___ closed clubface |
|  | ___ normal grip | ___ normal grip | ___ normal grip |
|  | ___ grip down 2 in. | ___ grip down 2 in. | ___ grip down 2 in. |
| Stance | ___ open | ___ square | ___ feet square or closed |
|  | ___ weight evenly distributed | ___ weight on left side | ___ weight on left side |
|  | ___ shoulders and hips open | ___ shoulders and hips square | ___ shoulders closed |
|  | ___ toes dug in sand | ___ toes dug in sand | ___ toes dug in sand |
| Ball Position | ___ slightly front of center | ___ 1 – 2 ball lengths back of center | ___ near right instep or back of center |
| Hands | ___ on a line in front of ball | ___ on a line in front of ball | ___ well ahead of ball |
| Backswing | ___ arms, hands, club move back as one unit | ___ steeper backswing, wrists hinge early, 3/4 swing length | ___ steep backswing, wrists hinge at the start of swing 1/2 – 3/4 swing length |
| Downswing | ___ weight shifts, arms, hands, and club move as a unit | ___ same as good lie | ___ steep path toward sand |
|  | ___ club contacts sand 2 – 4 inches behind ball | ___ same as good lie | ___ club contacts sand just behind ball |
|  | ___ accelerate through the sand | ___ same as good lie | ___ same as good lie |
| Follow-Through | ___ as long as backswing | ___ same as good lie | ___ not as long as backswing |
| Club | ___ sand wedge | ___ sand wedge | ___ pitching wedge |
| Score | _____ | _____ | _____ |
|  | 15 | 15 | 15 |

**FIGURE 7.26 Sand Shots Skill Builder Checklist**

## PLAY FROM DIRT

When your ball has stopped on dirt instead of the fairway, minor adjustments will get you back into play. Hard bare dirt is referred to as hardpan. Take a less lofted club so the sole does not bounce on the hard ground. You will also be able to swing slower and still get the ball the same distance, which you would not get from a full faster swing with a shorter club. If you have to use a sand wedge, square the clubface to the target line and place the ball back of center. Make a controlled, descending stroke. There is little room for error with this shot.

# 8

# BASIC RULES OF GOLF AND PLAYING PROCEDURES

The rules of golf are self-imposed. There are no officials, as in other sports, calling violations. The United States Golf Association (USGA) is the governing body for rules and play in the United States. The Royal and Ancient Golf Club of St. Andrews, Scotland, publishes rules that apply to international competition. A complete list of rules is available from the United States Golf Association. The rules of golf help all who play to compete in fairness. Golfers who are fair-minded will adhere to the rules at all times during play. While you are learning the game, understanding a few basic rules will help you enjoy the game. The handicapping system in golf allows players of all levels to compete fairly. In this chapter, you will learn how to establish a handicap and how it is used during play.

## Learner Skills

1. Demonstrate an understanding of the basic rules of golf and procedures for play.
2. Demonstrate an understanding of how to establish a handicap for amateur play.
3. Name the two major types of play.

## Prerequisite Skills

1. Understands the basic components of a golf hole and the course.

## RULES

The rules are designed to cover specific conditions and circumstances, which include: (1) equipment, (2) parts of the course, (3) types of competition, (4) procedures for play, (5) infractions and their penalties, (6) elements on the course that affect play, and (7) scoring.

### Equipment

The USGA rules state that a maximum of fourteen clubs may be carried during a round of golf. Partners may share clubs, but there cannot be more than fourteen clubs between the two players.

### Parts of the Course

**Putting Green.**   The putting green is all ground of a hole especially prepared for putting. A ball is said to be on the putting green when any part of it touches the putting green.

**Teeing Ground.**   The teeing ground is the starting place for the hole to be played. It is a rectangular area, two club lengths in depth, the front and sides of which are defined by the outside limits of two tee markers (Figure 8.1). A ball is outside the teeing ground when all of it lies outside the teeing ground.

**FIGURE 8.1    Teeing Ground.** Two club lengths in depth, the front and sides are determined by tee markers.

**Hazards.**    A hazard is any bunker or water hazard.

*Water Hazards.*    A water hazard is any sea, lake, pond, river, ditch, or open water, whether or not containing water, and anything of a similar nature. There will be two types of water hazards listed—the USGA Rule Book refers to a water hazard and a lateral water hazard—for purposes of explaining the procedures when golfers find their ball has come to rest in one.

WATER HAZARD (OTHER THAN A LATERAL HAZARD).    A water hazard is one that runs across the fairway (Figure 8.2). Some texts refer to these as direct water hazards, although the USGA does not use the term direct hazard. A water hazard is marked by yellow stakes and lines. These designate that the hazard is anywhere within these stakes. A ball is in the hazard when all or part of it rests in the boundaries marked by the stakes and lines.

LATERAL WATER HAZARD.    A lateral water hazard runs parallel to the fairway. Red stakes and lines are used to mark the boundaries of lateral water hazards. All markers and rules pertaining to the margins of the water hazard also apply to lateral water hazards.

*Bunker.*    A bunker is a hazard consisting of a prepared area of ground, usually a depression, from which turf or soil has been removed and replaced with sand. Grass cover bordering or within the bunker is not part of the bunker.

**FIGURE 8.2  Water Hazard**

*Ground Under Repair.*   Ground under repair is any portion of the golf course that is designated by stakes or white lines. The stakes and lines used to mark ground under repair are considered to be in such ground. When the ball touches the line, it is considered to be in ground under repair.

*Loose Impediments.*   Loose impediments are natural objects such as stones, leaves, twigs, branches, dung, worms, insects, or casts made by them. Loose impediments are not fixed, growing, or solidly imbedded; they do not adhere to the ball. Sand and loose soil are loose impediments only on the putting green. Snow and ice are either casual water or loose impediments, at the option of the player, except that manufactured ice is considered an obstruction. Dew is not considered a loose impediment.

*Casual Water.*   Casual water is any temporary accumulation of water on the course that is visible before or after the players take their stances and is not in a water hazard. Dew and frost are not casual water.

*Obstruction.*   An obstruction is anything artificial, including the artificial surfaces and sides of roads, paths and manufactured ice, except: (a) objects defining out of bounds, such as walls, fences, stakes, etc.; (b) any part of an immovable artificial object which is out of bounds; and (c) any construction declared to be an integral part of the course. Players are entitled to relief from obstructions. There are two types of obstructions: movable and immovable.

MOVABLE OBSTRUCTIONS.   Movable obstructions include things such as rakes, hoses, waste cans, and benches that are not fixed. These may be moved if the obstruction interferes with the player's stance or swing.

If the ball lies in or on the obstruction, the ball may be lifted and the obstruction moved. The ball shall then be dropped as near as possible to the spot directly under the place where the ball lay in or on the obstruction but not nearer the hole. An example is when your ball lands in a garbage can that is moveable.

IMMOVABLE OBSTRUCTION.   Immovable obstructions are objects that cannot be moved, such as sheds, houses, posts that are not out of bounds, fixed benches, water fountains, cart paths, and roads. If the ball lies in or on the obstruction or so close that the obstruction interferes with the player's stance or swing, the player is entitled to relief without penalty. The ball may be lifted and dropped within one club length of the ball's position. The point selected for dropping the ball may not be nearer the hole and may not be in a hazard or on a putting green.

## Types of Competition

There are two major types of play in the game of golf—match play and stroke play. Match Play: In match play, the objective is to shoot a lower score than your competition on each hole. So it is played hole by hole. The player who wins the most holes wins the match. Stroke Play: In stroke play, the objective is to shoot the lowest score for eighteen holes.

## Procedures for Play

**Out of Bounds.**    Out of bounds is the part of the course on which play is not permitted. Out of bounds may be defined by a fence, by stakes, or by a white line. When the out of bounds is defined by fences or stakes, a ball is considered out of bounds when all of it lies outside the nearest inside points of the stakes or fence posts at ground level. A player may stand out of bounds to hit a ball that is not out of bounds.

**Drop Procedure.**    Whenever a ball must be dropped, the player stands erect, holds the ball at shoulder height and arm's length and drops it (Figure 8.3). The player may face in any direction to drop the ball. If the dropped ball touches the player, the player's clothing, or equipment before or after it strikes the ground, the ball must be redropped. If the ball (1) rolls onto the green, (2) rolls out of bounds or into a hazard, or (3) rolls more than two club lengths from the marked drop point, the ball must be redropped. After the second drop, if the ball ends up in any of the three situations above, the ball may then be

**FIGURE 8.3   Drop Procedure**

placed. Except for paths and roads, the player may not cross over, under, or through an obstruction in determining a drop point.

**Teeing Off.** The following are basic procedures for the beginning of play. If you are in pairs or groups of three or four, you may flip a coin to decide who tees off first. The player or side teeing off first is said to "have the honor." After the first hole, the player with the lowest score on the previous hole tees off first on the remaining holes.

The ball may be placed on a tee, raised area on the ground, sand, or other substance to elevate the ball on the tee only. The player must play the ball within the tee markers. Tee markers may not be moved by the player if it is determined that the markers interfere with the player's stance. The player may stand outside the tee markers to make a stroke.

If a ball falls off the tee or the player knocks the ball off while addressing the ball, no penalty is incurred. A stroke is defined as the forward movement of the club made with the intention of striking the ball and moving the ball. If a player stops the swing before striking the ball, a stroke does not count. If a player swings and misses the ball after addressing the ball, it counts as a stroke and is called a whiff.

After all players in a group have teed off, the play continues with the person farthest from the hole playing next, and the one next farthest hitting second, until all are on the green. The person farthest from the hole putts first and so forth, until all have holed out their ball.

**On the Putting Green.** The line of putt is the line the player wishes his ball to take after a stroke is made on the putting green. The line of putt may not be touched except to move sand, soil, or other loose impediments. These may be brushed aside or picked up and removed with your hand or putter and nothing else. You cannot brush them away with a cap, for instance.

To repair a ball mark, use a tee or repair tool. Loosen the soil, (Figure 8.4), pull the turf toward the center of the mark, then smooth the turf with the putter head or by stepping on the spot. You cannot repair spike marks.

You may lift your ball off the green to clean it. Mark the spot before lifting the ball by placing a coin directly behind the ball. If your ball is in the way or on the line of another player's ball, you may move your ball either right or left. Ask the player in which direction the ball should be moved, then measure with the putter head, either right or left, and mark the spot at the heel of the putter (Figure 8.5).

**Flagstick.** The flagstick may be attended, removed, or held up by anyone, with the player's knowledge and if no objection is made. When the ball is off the green and you make a stroke, hitting the flagstick, there is no penalty unless you have authorized someone to attend it or hold it up to indicate where the hole is located. When addressing the ball, the player may place the putter

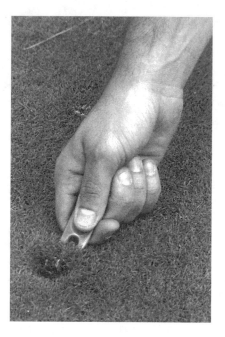

**FIGURE 8.4  Repair Ball Marks on the Green Using a Repair Tool.** Loosen soil and pull turf toward center.

**FIGURE 8.5  Marking Your Ball.** Players should mark and lift a ball that may interfere with play.

in front of the ball without pressing anything down. When making the putt, the player may not stand astride the intended line. The player must stand to the side.

**Ball on the Wrong Putting Green.**  If you are playing on a tight course where the fairways and greens are close together, your ball may land on the wrong green. If your ball lies on a putting green other than the hole being played, the point for dropping the ball should be on the course, off of the green, nearest to where the ball lies. It must not be nearer the hole being played and not in a hazard or on a putting green. The player may lift the ball and drop it without penalty within one club length of the point located for the drop. The drop point should be marked with a tee.

**Ball Interfering with or Assisting Play.**  Any player may lift his or her ball if it is determined that it might assist another player or interfere with play. The player may mark the ball's position and lift it out of the way or opt to play first. The ball is then replaced at the marked spot, not dropped.

## Scoring

Any violations of the rules of golf in certain situations result in penalty strokes. Penalty strokes consist of one or two strokes. In some cases, no penalties are incurred.

**No-Penalty Situations.** There are situations a player may encounter on the golf course during a round of play in which the ball may be played as it lies or relief is permitted. The player is entitled to relief if an obstacle interferes with the player's stance or swing. Situations in which a player may take relief without a penalty stroke include the following: (1) ball close to staked trees or shrubs; (2) holes made by burrowing animals; (3) their droppings; (4) ground under repair; (5) sprinkler heads; (6) casual water; (7) cart paths.

**One-Stroke Penalties.** The situations that result in one-stroke penalties include the following: (1) ball hit out of bounds; (2) ball resting in water hazards; (3) lost ball; (4) accidentally moving a ball; (5) unplayable lie.

*1. Out of Bounds.* When the ball is hit out of bounds, it may not be played from out of bounds. If a ball is declared out of bounds, it must be returned to the original spot where the ball was last hit, dropped, and a penalty stroke added to your score (Figure 8.6).

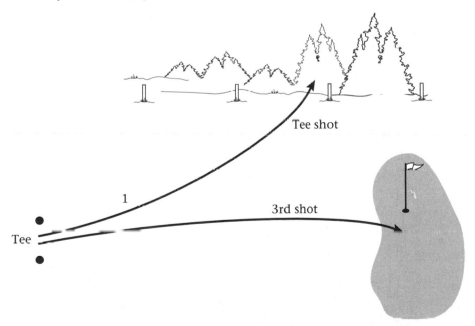

**FIGURE 8.6 Procedure for Out of Bounds.** Tee shot hit out of bounds: Return to tee, count first stroke, add penalty stroke, and hit your third shot. Out of bounds indicated by white stakes, white lines, or fences.

*2. Water Hazards.*

WATER HAZARD.   When a ball lands in a "direct" water hazard, there are several options open for playing the ball if the player decides not to play the ball from the hazard. You may not touch the ground in the hazard with your club until the downswing.

OPTION 1. Play the ball from the hazard.

OPTION 2. When a ball lands in a water hazard, other than a lateral water hazard, and is not played from the hazard, you may play another ball from the place where you played the first one, count strokes through the last shot, and take a penalty stroke. If your ball was played from the tee, you may retee the ball and play it.

OPTION 3. You may drop a ball behind the hazard, keeping the spot where the ball last crossed the margin of the hazard between the hole and the spot on which the ball is dropped. There is no limit to how far behind the water hazard the ball may be dropped. Count the strokes through the shot and add a penalty stroke. Figure 8.7 illustrates the procedures for a ball in a water hazard.

LATERAL WATER HAZARD (Figure 8.8).

OPTION 1. You may choose to play the ball as it lies without penalty.

OPTION 2. Return to the original spot, drop another ball, and add a penalty stroke to the strokes through the last shot.

OPTION 3. Determine where the ball last crossed the margin of the hazard. Drop a ball outside the hazard within two club lengths of the point where the ball last crossed the margin of the hazard, no closer to the hole. Add a penalty stroke to your score.

OPTION 4. Go to the other side of the hazard to a point directly opposite the point where the ball last crossed the margin of the hazard, equidistant from the hole. Drop a ball outside the hazard within two club lengths of the point where the ball crossed the margin of the hazard, no closer to the hole. Add a penalty stroke to your score.

OPTION 5. Drop from behind the hazard on a line formed by the hole and point where the ball entered the hazard. There is no limit on how far back you may drop the ball. Add a penalty stroke to your score.

*3. Lost Ball.*   A ball is lost if it is not found within 5 minutes after a player has begun to search for it. When the player declares that the ball is lost, another ball must be dropped at the point from which the original ball was hit or if hit from the tee, the ball must be reteed. Count the strokes through that shot and add a penalty stroke. If the player decides to hit a provisional ball, it becomes the ball in play if the lost ball is not found. If the player hits the provisional ball, then finds the original ball, the provisional ball must be the one played.

*4. Ball Accidentally Moved.*   A ball in play that is accidentally moved by a player addressing the ball or removing loose impediments through the green results in a one-stroke penalty.

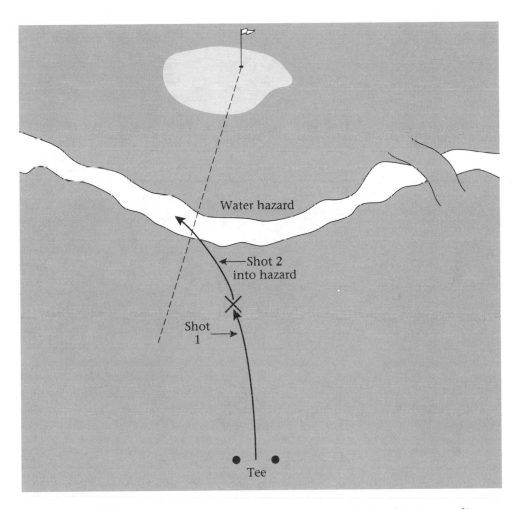

**FIGURE 8.7   Procedures for a Water Hazard.** Second shot hit into a direct hazard. *Option 1:* Play the ball from the hazard without a  penalty. *Option 2:* Drop at "x" where the second shot was made. Add a penalty stroke and play shot 4. *Option 3:* Drop a ball any distance behind the hazard. Keep the point at which the ball last crossed the margin of the hazard between the hole and the spot on which the ball is dropped. Count shot 2 plus a penalty stroke and hit shot 4.

*5. Unplayable Lie.*   There are situations in which a player may decide that the ball is unplayable. For example, a ball may land in a tree stump or in thick bushes or heavy rocks. A player may declare that the ball is unplayable anywhere on the course, as long as the ball does not lie in or touch a water hazard. There are three methods for taking relief when the ball is declared unplayable.

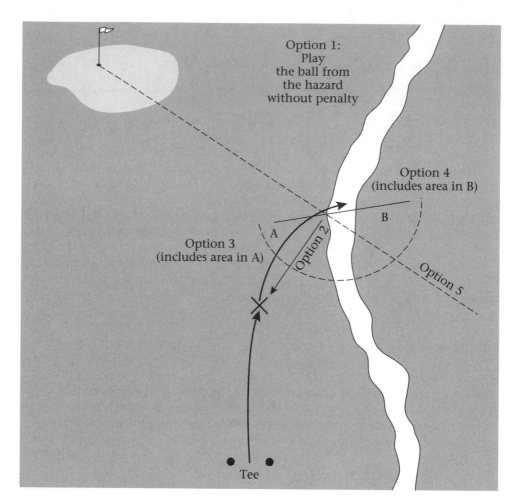

**FIGURE 8.8  Procedure for Lateral Water Hazard.** *Options:* (1) Play original ball from hazard without penalty. (2) Return to where the second shot was hit, drop a ball, count shot 2, add a penalty stroke and hit shot 4. (3 and 4) Drop the ball within two club lengths of where the ball crossed the margin of the hazard or a point equidistant from the hole on the opposite margin of the hazard. Count shot 2 plus a penalty stroke and hit shot 4. (5) Drop a ball under penalty of one stroke anywhere on a line behind the hazard, keeping the point where the ball crossed the hazard between the hole and the drop point. Count shot 2 plus a penalty stroke and hit shot 4.

**Method 1.** Go back to the original spot, drop and hit another ball. If the ball was on the tee, it may be reteed. Count the strokes through the shot and add a penalty stroke.

**Method 2.** Drop a ball within two club lengths of where the ball lay but no closer to the hole. Add a penalty stroke to the strokes through the shot.

**Method 3.** Move back on a line as far as desired, keeping the declared unplayable point between the spot on which the ball is dropped and the hole. Add a penalty stroke to the stroke or strokes through the last shot.

**Two-Stroke Penalties.** Certain situations may result in two-stroke penalties. These situations include: (1) hitting the wrong ball; (2) hitting the flagstick or another player's ball when putting from on the green; (3) grounding a club in a hazard; (4) asking for advice. Players should easily avoid two-stroke penalty infractions.

1. Wrong Ball. Hitting the wrong ball must be corrected before the player tees off on the next hole or before leaving the green on the last hole of a round. If the mistake is not corrected before teeing off on the next tee or leaving the last green of the last hole, the player is disqualified. Always mark your ball with a waterproof marker. Count the strokes up to hitting the wrong ball and add two penalty strokes. Strokes played with a wrong ball do not count on the player's score.

2. Flagstick/Another Player's Ball. Hitting the flagstick or another player's ball while trying to hole out from on the putting green results in a two-stroke penalty. You should request that a ball be marked and lifted if you think it is in your way. If you do hit another player's ball, play your ball from where it lies. The other player's ball should be replaced in the position it was before it was hit.

3. Grounding The Club. Grounding the club, or placing the sole on the ground in a hazard before the downswing, results in a two-stroke penalty. Take your practice swings outside the hazard.

4. Advice Or Assistance. Advice is any suggestion that might influence a player in choosing a club, the means for making a stroke, or how to make a shot. For example, you may not ask which club to use or request help with your swing. You may not have assistance, such as physical protection from the rain, while making a stroke. You may ask things such as the distance from a permanent object to the center of the green or the length of a hole.

**Penalty Stroke Summary.** Sometimes it is difficult to remember what counts as a one- or two-stroke penalty. Figure 8.9 summarizes penalty strokes situations.

| No Penalty | One-Stroke Penalties | Two-Stroke Penalties |
|---|---|---|
| casual water | accidentally move a ball | requesting advice ("What club should I use on this shot?") |
| holes, droppings by animals | ball is lost | |
| | out of bounds | |
| sprinkler heads | water hazard | hitting the wrong ball |
| ground under repair (must be marked) | unplayable lie | grounding a club in a hazard |
| staked trees, shrubs | whiffing the ball (make a stroke and miss the ball) | hitting a ball or flag when putting on the green |

**FIGURE 8.9    Penalty Stroke Summary**

## HANDICAP SYSTEM

Many amateur golfers do not shoot par golf. A system of establishing an individual handicap in golf allows players of all levels and abilities to compete against each other fairly. A handicap is easy to establish through a local club or golf association. Simply turn in your scores for eighteen holes at your local club. After about ten to fifteen scores are received, for a small fee your handicap can be established. You will receive a card to use to show your official handicap.

The USGA rates golf courses based on the difficulty of the course. Usually, the rating is very near par for the particular golf course. Your handicap is computed by averaging your lowest ten scores against the established rating for the course or courses on which they were shot. A percentage of this difference is calculated and becomes your established handicap.

### How Does the Handicap Work during Play?

If you score on the average of around 95 for eighteen holes, your handicap will be about 18 to 20. Suppose that two players, Dan and Jill, want to compete against each other for eighteen holes. Dan has a handicap of 24, and Jill's handicap is 12. The difference between the two players' handicaps is 12. Dan will be given 12 strokes off his score. These strokes will be taken off his gross score on the holes ranked 1 to 12 on the scorecard (holes are rated by difficulty). Note on the Ironwood Golf Course scorecard how Jill and Dan keep their scores (Figure 8.10). Dan's 12 strokes are indicated by a dot. He will have a stroke subtracted from his score on each of these holes, giving him a net score. So on hole one, if Dan and Jill both get a bogey (5), Dan will get a stroke subtracted and receive a net score of 4 for the first hole.

**Rule Skill Builders**

PENALTY AND PROCEDURES DRILL

*Purpose:* To determine the penalty and procedures for specific situations encountered during play.

*Equipment:* picture of a hole with bunkers and water hazards

*Activity:* Answer the following questions for each situation:

    **a.** What are the procedures for playing the next shot in each situation?
    **b.** What is/are the penalty stroke/s?
    **c.** How many strokes will the player have after playing the next shot?

1. You have discovered that on your second shot from the short rough, near the edge of the fairway, you have played the wrong ball.

    Procedure? _____

    Penalty? _____

    Total strokes after penalty and next shot? _____

2. Your ball rolls to a stop on a cart path after your second shot.

    Procedure? _____

    Penalty? _____

    Total strokes after penalty and next shot? _____

3. You have hit your tee shot into high rough on the right and after 5 minutes of searching cannot find it.

    Procedure? _____

    Penalty? _____

    Total strokes after penalty and next shot? _____

4. You are in the middle of the fairway. As you set up to hit your third shot, you discover that you are standing on the raised edge of a mole's tunnel.

    Procedure? _____

    Penalty? _____

    Total strokes after penalty and next shot? _____

5. You are chipping with your third stroke onto the green and hit the flagstick. Your ball bounces off the flagstick and hits another player's ball, knocking it off the green. Your ball stays on the edge of the green.

    Procedure? _____

    Penalty? _____

    Total strokes after penalty and next shot? _____

*Continued*

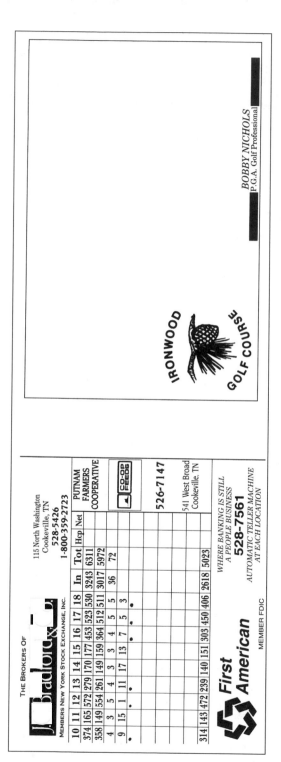

## Ironwood Golf Course Scorecard

### The Brokers of J. Bradford & Co.
MEMBERS NEW YORK STOCK EXCHANGE, INC.

| 10 | 11 | 12 | 13 | 14 | 15 | 16 | 17 | 18 | In | Tot | Hcp | Net |
|----|----|----|----|----|----|----|----|----|----|-----|-----|-----|
| 374 | 165 | 572 | 279 | 170 | 177 | 453 | 523 | 530 | 3243 | 6311 | | |
| 358 | 149 | 554 | 261 | 149 | 159 | 364 | 512 | 511 | 3017 | 5972 | | |
| 4 | 3 | 5 | 4 | 3 | 3 | 5 | 5 | 5 | 36 | 72 | | |
| 9 | 15 | 1 | 11 | 17 | 13 | 7 | 5 | 3 | | | | |
| | | • | | | | • | • | • | | | | |
| | | | | | | | • | • | | | | |
| 314 | 143 | 472 | 239 | 140 | 151 | 303 | 450 | 406 | 2618 | 5023 | | |

115 North Washington
Cookeville, TN
528-5426
1-800-359-2723

PUTNAM FARMERS COOPERATIVE

CO-OP FEEDS

526-7147

541 West Broad
Cookeville, TN

### First American
WHERE BANKING IS STILL
A PEOPLE BUSINESS
528-7561
AUTOMATIC TELLER MACHINE
AT EACH LOCATION
MEMBER FDIC

**IRONWOOD GOLF COURSE**

*BOBBY NICHOLS*
P.G.A. Golf Professional

---

### Cody Office Supply
Business People Serving
Business People
450 South Jefferson
Cookeville, TN 38501
526-7131

| Hole | 1 | 2 | 3 | 4 | 5 | 6 | 7 | 8 | 9 | Out |
|------|----|----|----|----|----|----|----|----|----|-----|
| Championship | 365 | 153 | 398 | 337 | 411 | 314 | 142 | 505 | 443 | 3068 |
| Regular | 353 | 141 | 385 | 327 | 399 | 301 | 134 | 488 | 427 | 2955 |
| Par | 4 | 3 | 4 | 4 | 4 | 4 | 3 | 5 | 5 | 36 |
| Handicap | 10 | 16 | 8 | 12 | 6 | 14 | 18 | 2 | 4 | |
| Jill | | • | | • | • | | | | • | |
| Dan | • | | | | | | | • | | |
| Ladies' | 316 | 131 | 335 | 282 | 322 | 247 | 126 | 337 | 309 | 2405 |

### Legge Insurance Agency

### Burger King
Get your
burger's worth.™
957 South Jefferson
250 West Spring Street

Valley Ford
(need copy)

W.R. Whitaker
& Company
537-6514
537-6515
Cookeville, TN 38506

Coors
LIGHT
Coors
COORS
IS THE
ONE

---

### Coca-Cola of Cookeville

### Great Day Chiropractic
Dr. Roseanne Ellis
*Gentle and Effective*
Pain Relief • Correction • Wellness • Physical Therapy
Most Insurance Accepted
Status at Cookeville General Hospital
135 W. Jackson, Cookeville 528-8362
207 W. Commercial St. Monterey 839-3337

| Slope | |
|-------|------|
| Ladies' | 112 |
| Men | |
| Front | 119 |
| Back | 123 |

| Course Rating | |
|---------------|------|
| Championship: | 70.7 |
| Regular: | 68.9 |
| Ladies': | 68.5 |

**RULES OF PLAY**
1. U.S.G.A. rules apply except where modified by local rules.
2. No more than fivesomes at any time.
3. Glass containers not permitted on golf course.
4. All golfers must wear shirts.
5. No children under 16 may operate golf carts.
6. No two golfers may play from same bag.
Please repair all ball marks.
Be courteous—Let 'em through.
Please replace divots.

Date: _____
Scorer: _____
Attest: _____

### Cumberland Gold Jewelry
Market Square
528-1074
*Tim Koehler, Owner*

CLUBHOUSE &
PRO SHOP
PARKING

## FIGURE 8.10  Handicap Play

130

*Continued*

6. You hit your second shot, and it stops under a rake along the edge, but not in, a greenside bunker.

    Procedure? _____    _____

    Penalty? _____

    Total strokes after penalty and next shot? _____

7. You hit your second shot into a lateral water hazard.

    Procedure? _____    _____

    Penalty? _____    _____

    Total strokes after penalty and next shot? _____

# 9

# ETIQUETTE AND SAFETY
# ON THE COURSE

This chapter will discuss etiquette procedures and safety precautions to be applied on the golf course and while attending a professional golf tournament. Etiquette refers to the player's adherence to correct behavior during a round of golf or while viewing a live round. Traditionally, golf has been a game of honesty and courtesy. Poor behavior on the course or while watching a tournament simply is not accepted. Good golfers appreciate another player who demonstrates proper etiquette and safety precautions, even if that person does not play the game well. One of the best things you can do for your golf game is to learn and practice proper etiquette and safety.

## Learner Skills

1. Demonstrate an understanding of golf etiquette while playing or attending a tournament.
2. Demonstrate an understanding of safety procedures during a round of play or on the range.

## Prerequisite Skills

1. Understands the structure of a golf course.
2. Understands the concept of how a round of golf is played.
3. Understands or has some concept of the ability to control one's temper and emotional state.

## PERSONAL CONDUCT

Golf is a game of highs and lows. All kinds of circumstances will arise to test a golfer's patience and emotions. The following are suggestions for conduct on the course. Be courteous to all players and treat them as you would want to be treated. Be quiet when other players are making their shots. Stand far enough away and to the side of players so that you do not interfere with the shot. Refrain from emotional outbursts when you execute a poor shot. Just accept that play will not always be perfect. You will make mistakes and feel frustrated at times. Help other golfers look for a lost ball. Do not critique a player's skill during a round of play or try to give advice on improvement.

If a course has a dress code, by all means abide by it. Most courses require slacks, shorts of appropriate length, some form of knit shirt, or a reasonable tee shirt. Tank tops and gym-style shorts are often not allowed on golf courses. Baseball and track shoes are not allowed. Athletic or golf shoes (spike or spikeless versions) are the preferred type of shoe.

### Care of the Course

Golf courses cost enormous amounts of money to build and maintain. Players, especially after paying a green fee, want to play on a course that is not full of divots taken out of the fairway or ball marks left on a green. Golfers should take care of the course and leave it better than when they found it. The following procedures will help assure that you leave the course in good repair.

**Litter.**   Place all litter in appropriate containers. If you see a can or paper on the course, pick it up or put it in a container.

**Golf Carts.**   Drive golf carts on designated paths, avoiding areas close to the green. Most courses mark the area around the green with small signs to direct carts, or the areas may be roped. Carts should not be driven over tees, greens, or in bunkers.

When a course is wet from too much rain, usually a 90-degree rule is implemented. This means to stay on the cart path until you arrive at your ball. Then you can drive onto the fairway in a straight line toward your ball. When the course is very wet, the rule will be to stay on cart paths only. Always ask the pro shop personnel or the starter what the cart rule for the day is.

Pull carts and golf bags should be kept off the green, out of bunkers, and off the tees, Place golf bags and pull carts between the green and next tee before putting. Figure 9.1 illustrates a bag that is placed too close to the green.

**Divot Repair.**   Replace divots made with the club by retrieving them and placing them back in the indention made in the soil. After replacing the divot,

**FIGURE 9.1   Where to Position Bags Around the Green.** The bag at the top of the photo is too close to the green. The bag at the bottom is better placed between the green and the next tee.

**FIGURE 9.2   Care of Bunkers** Rake your footprints, club, and ball marks.

tap it down with your foot. Leave your club laying next to the indention so you will know where to replace the divot.

**Bunker Repair.**   After making a sand shot, rake the sand in bunkers, smoothing your foot and club prints (Figure 9.2). Enter the bunker at the point nearest your ball, taking the rake with you, placing it out of the way as you make the shot. Replace the rake outside the bunker with the sharp side facing down. Be sure to move the rake if it is in your way, as you are entitled to relief from movable obstructions (Figure 9.2).

## Keeping the Pace of Play

Golf requires concentration and play at a continual pace. Good and experienced golfers tend to get into a rhythm of play and do not like to have their pace interrupted by slow play. There are many things that golfers, even inexperienced ones, can do to keep the pace of play continual. You should be able to complete an eighteen-hole round within four hours.

**Saving Time.**   If your partner's ball is on one side of the fairway and yours is on the other, get the clubs you think you will need and walk to your ball. If you take only a 7-iron and discover you really need a 5-iron, you will have to return to the cart to get another club. What really slows play is when you sit in the cart, watch your partner hit, then both drive to your ball, decide what club to use, then get out of the cart to hit. Another option to speed play is to let your partner get the club needed, then drive the cart to your ball if it is not in the way in the fairway. Your group can adopt a procedure on the tee that allows players to hit when they are ready instead of following the usual hitting procedures. The same is true in the fairway and on the green. Always be ready to hit when it is your turn. Be selecting the shot and the club you need while others are hitting. Do not take more than one practice swing.

**Playing Through.**   If a hole is open or has no players ahead of you, let the group behind you play through if they appear to be playing at a faster pace than your group. To allow players to play through, be sure it is clear ahead of your group, wave the group behind you to play through, then step to one side of the fairway and wait for them to hit. Be sure to thank others when they let your group play through. To avoid congestion on par threes, allow the group waiting to hit up to the green with your group.

**Watch Your Ball.**   Always follow the flight of your golf ball, even if it is a shot you do not like or even want to see. This will help you identify a landmark that will lead you to your ball and save time. If you see that your ball might be lost or out of bounds, hit a "provisional ball." Also, watch your partner's ball.

**Playing the Hazards.**   If a water hazard is in front of you, you have hit two balls in the hazard already, and there is a group behind you, pick up and hit from the other side of the hazard in a friendly game. No one really cares about your golf score if it is already 40 and you are only on hole six of a round. If you are playing out of a fairway bunker and you are on your third or fourth try to get out of the bunker, pick up your ball and toss it in the fairway or stop playing the hole if you are having a friendly round. You will be more relaxed, and the group behind you will be a lot happier. Tee off on the next hole. You will have time to get it together after the exasperating bunker experience.

## Procedures on the Green

The person closest to the pin should attend it or remove it when all are ready to putt. The person who holes out last should replace the flagstick when all have putted. The flagstick should be replaced and removed gently—lay it down instead of dropping it to the green—so the turf around the hole is not jabbed, dented, or torn. Place any extra club, such as your pitching wedge, at a spot between the green and the next tee. This will save time after you have putted, as you will not have to go back across the green to get the extra club.

Do not let your shadow fall on another player's line of putt (Figure 9.3). Do not stand or walk on another player's line of putt. Stand so that you do not distract the person putting—to the side of the person is probably best. If your putt is on the same line as another player's, watch the break or what the ball does to give you an idea of the putt. You will not have to spend as much time reading the green. You can be lining up your putt if you do not interfere with a player who is putting. This will save time.

Leave the green immediately, recording scores for the hole near the next tee, never on the green. Do not make extra putts to practice after all have holed out if others are waiting to approach the green. If you get to the next tee and others are putting, remain quiet until they are through.

Remember, you will be remembered more for your etiquette than your golf score. Most likely you will be invited back to play by other golfers.

Do not damage newly planted staked trees or shrubs on the course. If your ball is so close that your swing will damage the new shrub, you are entitled to relief and may drop your ball away from the shrub so that the ball is no closer to the hole.

**FIGURE 9.3    Putting Etiquette.**
Do not walk on another player's
line of putt or let your shadow
get in the way.

## ETIQUETTE WHILE ATTENDING A GOLF TOURNAMENT

Professional, or even collegiate, golf tournaments, are fun to watch in person. However, there are etiquette procedures that should be followed at these events. These suggestions will allow the competitors to concentrate on their game without interference from the crowds.

1. Always be quiet when someone is ready to hit. Usually the marshal will hold a hand in the air to signal you. Some will have signs that say "quiet," especially around the putting green. If you are next to the putting green, wait until all in the group have putted out before you move to the next tee or away from the green.
2. It is not polite to yell out as if you were at a football game. A nice hand clap is enough when a player makes a shot that you like.
3. Do not ask for autographs until a player is finished with the round. Most will give autographs during a practice round before the tournament. If you want a player's autograph, you will stand a better chance if you bring a marking pen and whatever you wish to be signed by the player. Players may walk while signing their names, so walk along with them. Be sure to say thank you.
4. Cameras, VCRs, beepers, cellular phones, or other electronic devices are not allowed during the actual tournament rounds. These can be brought to the practice rounds.
5. Avoid letting the portable restroom doors slam shut.
6. It is probably best to leave small children and pets at home. Small children tire easily and limit your activity.

## SAFETY PROCEDURES DURING A ROUND OF GOLF

A golf ball traveling at speeds of 80 to 100 miles per hour can do serious damage if it hits someone. It is up to each player to be aware of others on the course. Safety procedures should always be practiced during play. At professional events it is up to the spectator to practice safety precautions.

### Safety during Play

Look around for others and obstructions before taking practice swings. Do not walk or stand behind someone ready to swing. You do not want to get hurt nor do you want to hurt anybody. It is best to bring small children to the course only when it is not crowded.

## Golf Cart Safety

Never let children under age fourteen drive a powered golf cart. Ride two persons only on a powered golf cart. Sit well into the cart, as it has no seat belts. Start slowly and make turns cautiously. Always use the parking break on the golf cart. Do not get out of the cart or try to hop on until it comes to a complete stop. Drive carefully.

## Know What Is Ahead

When a hole or fairway cannot be seen because of a curve or hill, be sure to check to see that players are not in your hitting range. Wait until players are well ahead of your hitting range before you hit. If you should accidentally hit toward or into a group ahead of you or into a group in an adjacent fairway, yell the warning cry "Fore." This is one time when you should not be shy to yell loudly. If you hear "fore," duck, cover your head, and do not turn around.

If you hit into another fairway, allow the players in that fairway to play their shots before you hit. Look carefully before entering another fairway to find your ball.

## Lightning!

Lightning is extremely dangerous on the golf course. Player or spectator, lightning does not know the difference. So all are in danger. Watch the sky and if you see lightning moving toward you, try first to get off the course. If it is too late, take shelter in deep woods but never under one or two trees. Put your clubs and umbrella away—they are lightning rods.

If deep woods are not around, lie in a depression or low spot on the ground, or just lie flat if nothing else can be done. Many professional events have designated lightning shelters. Learn where they are and use them. Golf courses usually have procedures posted on golf carts or in the pro shop for what to do if there is lightning. They will also have a warning signal when lightning is in the immediate area. The signal is usually a siren noise. When you hear it, leave the course immediately and head for the pro shop or a shelter.

## Play during Weather Extremes

Play in the summer usually means playing on hot humid days. It is important to keep hydrated during play. Drink water, about a quarter cup on each hole, especially if you are walking. Avoid alcohol as it dehydrates the body.

Keeping a wet towel around your neck helps to keep you cool. Try to stay in the shade as much as possible. Always use sun screen, one that has a protection factor of at least SPF 15 or more. Wear a hat or visor to keep the sun off your face. If at all possible, play early in the morning, before 11 o'clock, or after 2 o'clock in the afternoon.

Play during very cold weather is possible. Wear light layers of clothing instead of two heavy pieces. Top the layers off with a wind breaker type of jacket. Protect your feet by wearing two pair of socks. A ski mask also adds protection to your face and ears. A hat is a must. Remember to protect your hands. Winter golf gloves help. It is better to walk in the winter if you can. Some carts have wind breakers, but wind added to cold air makes it colder. Carry a warm drink in a thermos. Avoid alcohol while playing in the cold.

## Nutrition

If you are out for a day of golfing, proper nutrition will help you fight fatigue and maintain your energy level. Try to eat a good meal before playing, one that is mostly protein and carbohydrates. Carry along a snack of fruit, dry cereal, or nuts. Avoid high sugar foods and a lot of caffeine. You will get a sugar or caffeine high and then a sluggish low. Sports drinks, water, and fruit juices are better for you than alcohol. Save the alcohol for after your round if you want to have a drink.

---

**Etiquette and Safety Skill Builders**

SPEED UP PLAY DRILL

*Purpose:* To help the player develop strategies for speeding up play

*Equipment:* none

*Activity:*

1. Determine three strategies for speeding up play for the following situation. You have hit your ball on the right edge of the fairway 25 yards ahead of your partner, who is on the left edge of the fairway. You are to keep the carts on the cart path during round of play. How can play be speeded up in this situation?

   _____

   _____

2. A group behind you and your partner has been waiting on the second hole. The next hole is a par 3, and there is a group teeing off on the next hole. What should you do to speed up play?

   _____

LEAVING THE COURSE BETTER THAN YOU FOUND IT

What are three things you can do to leave the course better than you found it?

_____

*Continued*

*Continued*

SAFETY

What are three options you have to protect yourself if caught in a lightning storm?

_____

_____

_____

What is the warning cry in golf that means that a ball is coming toward you? _____

What are at least three safety precautions for operating a golf cart?

_____

_____

_____

Describe some safety precautions for playing in the heat.

_____

PLAYING THROUGH

What are three safe steps for letting a group behind you play through?

_____

_____

_____

# 10

## PLAYING YOUR FIRST
## ROUND OF GOLF

Playing your first round of golf requires more than just the physical aspects; it also requires mental preparation. Once you feel reasonably confident that you can execute the basic skills of golf, it will be time to try them out on the course. Mental aspects of play require the ability to concentrate on the task at hand, reduce tension, feel confident, execute the shot, and control your emotions.

Course management of your first round will require some planning and strategy for playing each hole. Obviously, each golfer will have strengths and weaknesses that include mental characteristics, how each club is hit, what type of shot pattern is produced (slices, hooks), the distance each club is hit, which skills are best, and which ones are weaker. This chapter will help you prepare for your first round of golf and strategies for managing your emotions as you play.

### Learner Skills

1. Demonstrate an awareness of the mental aspects of play—confidence, concentration. emotional and tension control.
2. Select strategies for relaxing, controlling emotions, concentration, and developing confidence.
3. Given a particular golf hole, identify the hole's strengths and weaknesses.
4. Use the procedures for starting a round of golf.

### Prerequisite Skills

1. Understands the physical features of a golf hole and typical course layout.
2. Understands the purpose and use of each club—wood, iron, putter.
3. Knows the basic rules and etiquette of golf.
4. Demonstrates some competence at the full swing, chip and pitch shots, putting, play from the rough, and uneven lies.

## DEVELOPING CONFIDENCE

Great golfers did not get where they are without having a lot of confidence. One important way that most of us develop self-confidence is through our dialogue with ourselves. Many beginning golfers or high-handicap players use negative self-talk when they make a bad shot. They call themselves stupid or other negative descriptors and feel embarrassed.

Golfers must believe in themselves. Positive self-talk might sound like this: "I have made this shot before. I have practiced it. Therefore, I know I can make it." If you do make a bad shot, put it in perspective. It is only one shot of at least 85 or 90 strokes in a round of golf.

### Building Self-Confidence

Some tips for developing self-confidence include the following: During instruction or a round of golf, focus on what you did well rather than the poorer aspects of play and practice. If you catch yourself making negative statements, change them to positive ones. Believe that you can make every shot you attempt. Practice improving your weaknesses. Play with people who build your self-esteem. Avoid those who try to undermine you. Focus on the positives and all the possibilities. "There is a lot of room on the right side of the fairway," instead of "Oh, no. Look at all the water on the left." "If I really concentrate, I can make this putt," instead of "I am not very good at long putts; I always leave them short." Start your first rounds of golf feeling confident.

## MENTAL CHARACTERISTICS

### Motivation

A strong desire to achieve and finish tasks relates to motivation. One way to help motivation is to create goals. Goals then, in turn, motivate us into action. Setting goals that are too high and therefore not reached results in discouragement. Set reachable goals and commit to achieving them. Here is an example: Suppose, as a beginner, you want to be better at chipping. You have had two class periods of instruction on chipping. One afternoon, you decide to practice chipping. A nonproductive way is to get some golf balls, an 8-iron, stand around the green and chip away for half an hour, and leave. What have you accomplished? You probably do not know, because you had no particular goal in mind.

A more productive way would have been to set at least one goal with objectives that could be measured to see if progress was being made. Here is an example related to chipping.

**Goal.**　Improve chipping accuracy from longer distances between 5 and 10 yards.

**Objective.**   From a distance of 3 yards from the edge of the green, chip five out of ten balls so they stop within 5 feet of the hole. When you have accomplished this objective, increase the level of difficulty. Try to chip six out of ten balls from a longer distance so they land within 5 feet of the hole. With a goal in mind and a way to measure it, you can see progress. This builds confidence and keeps motivation high.

Trust the skills you have and play within those skills. Keep the ball in play and make progress toward the green. It might be better not to try to keep score for a while as you play those first rounds. Set your own par for each hole. Suppose that a double bogey (2 over par) is about the best you can do at this point. Be satisfied and enjoy making double bogeys until you become more skilled through lessons and practice.

Play what works for you and the skills you have developed to that point. Your partners may be hitting drivers straight down the middle. But if you can hit a 3-wood down the middle rather than the driver, use the 3-wood; you will be better off, with a fairway shot to the green instead of some difficult situation.

Figure 10.1 includes a goal mastery sheet for different aspects of your golf game. These may be used to establish goals and measurable objectives and to

| Skill | Goal | Objective | Date |
|---|---|---|---|
| Putting | | | |
| Chipping | | | |
| Pitching | | | |
| Full Swing | | | |
| Sand shots | | | |
| Pre-Shot Routine | | | |
| Rules | | | |
| Etiquette | | | |

**FIGURE 10.1   Goal Mastery for Skills**

record the date when the goals were achieved. This approach to your game will allow you to have a better time as you play your first few rounds of golf.

## Controlling Emotions

All kinds of conditions occur during a round of golf. The weather can change from sunny and warm to wet and cool; other players can slow play; or the wind speed can change. You cannot control these circumstances, but you can control how you react to them. Examining your emotional reactions to changing conditions will help you learn to control how you react to conditions during a round of play. The following strategies will help you deal with conditions that affect your round, especially those first few that you play.

- Realize that certain conditions that happen you cannot change.
- Focus on yourself. Forget about others and their game. Concentrate on the things you can control—how you think, your self-talk, and how you react to situations.
- Keep calm and control tension. Emotional outbursts and letting situations upset you only add tension, which is disastrous to a golf swing. Would you want to play with someone who was cursing, yelling, and throwing clubs?
- Focus on the here and now. Avoid thinking about the next hole or what happened on the last hole. Avoid comparing yourself to other golfers, either your partners or others you see in other fairways.
- Be patient. You will not hit every shot perfectly. Recover from these less than perfect shots by being calm, patient, and confident. Especially be patient. Some individuals try to hit a career shot on each hole. Most often they end up in trouble, either out of bounds or in the water.

## Recognizing Tension and Controlling Strategies

Tension can create a real disaster for a golf swing. Some signs of tension during the golf swing include a tight grip with white knuckles showing, tightness in your shoulders and neck, and shot errors such as topping the ball, slices, fat shots.

Tension control strategies can be applied during a round of play to bring about a more relaxed state. Several of these strategies include the following.

1. Relax the muscles. Tighten your fists. Then tense all the muscles of your body. Hold for 5 or 10 seconds, then release. Repeat this two or three times while waiting to tee off or while golfers ahead of you are making their shots.
2. Golf courses are in some of the most beautiful real estate you will find. Look around and enjoy the view.
3. Control tension-producing thoughts. The following are examples of tension-producing thoughts and tension-reduction thoughts:

Tension-Producing Thoughts: "Play is slow. That really interrupts my tempo. This round is ruined, the day is ruined." "I hate waiting. It makes me nervous."

Tension-Reducing Thoughts: "Play is slow, but I will have time to enjoy the scenery." "I have time to really think about each shot now and be more selective." "The sun feels so good and it is such a nice day." "How fortunate I am to be able to play golf today."

## READY TO PLAY

Now that you are aware of mental skills you will need for your first round, remember to take them to the course and use them. Being prepared to play is important and one of the first steps to a successful and pleasant round. There are certain things you can do to prepare yourself.

### Equipment

Check your equipment and golf bag before you leave for the course. If your clubs are full of mud, clean them. Do you have the following: tees, ball mark repair tool, golf balls (at least a half dozen), towel, sun screen, ball mark, and (optional) golf shoes, glove, visor, and umbrella?

### Tee Time

Call the pro shop where you intend to play and make a tee time if one is required. Most busy courses require tee times. Let them know if you will be alone or with others. Most of the time, four players are allowed to play together, especially during peak hours.

Try to schedule a tee time when the course is not so crowded—late afternoon on the weekend, mornings during the week. If you are not sure, ask when the course is the least crowded. If you are by yourself, be prepared to be placed with another player or group, which is a great opportunity to meet new people and make new friends.

When you arrive, check in at the pro shop to let them know you are there. If your partners are there, inform them of your arrival. Get a score card and pencil.

### Warming Up

Try to get there at least 30 minutes before your tee time. Get a small bucket of balls and go to the range. Take all of your clubs. First, do some stretching. Hit five balls with a wedge or 9-iron, then with a 7-iron and a long iron. Hit a few wood shots, using a 3-wood. You might end with the club you think you will use on the first tee. Visualize the tee shot and practice making that shot.

Go to the practice green and hit a few chip shots, then putt from a long distance a few times to get a feel for the greens. End up with three short successful putts. You should feel warmed up, relaxed, confident, and ready to go.

If you do arrive with only a few minutes before you must begin play, be sure to do some stretching and warm-up. Slowly swing a couple of clubs at the same time. Putt a few long and short putts.

## First Shot

Your first tee shot should be made with an easy swing. Remember, it is important to begin that first shot with success. This will set the tone for the rest of the hole and even the rest of the round. Have a key swing thought in mind, such as, "Finish the swing" or "coil and uncoil."

## Tee Markers

Sometimes the tee markers will not line up with the middle of the fairway. Be sure to find a target and do not rely on the tee markers to align you. If there is water or other hazard on one side, it is best to line up on that side and hit away from it. You must play the same tees throughout the round.

## Course Management

During a round of golf, how well you manage the course impacts your score. As well as preparing to play, the mental aspects of controlling your reactions to conditions have been discussed. Once on the course and during play, your strategy for play is also important. These elements include concentration, gathering facts to make the shot selection, and going through a good pre-shot routine.

## Focus

Concentration on the task at hand helps keep you focused. In golf, the task is to select a shot and execute it without being distracted. The time to focus does not begin when you stand over the ball to make the shot. It should begin before that point. Concentration should begin when you get near your ball. Some players like to begin concentrating when they are within 20 yards of their ball. Some stay focused from tee to green, especially in competitive golf. This is when you turn on your radar to scope out the situation. You start gathering facts for the shot selection. Following are steps to help you concentrate and focus on the shot.

- Begin to filter out conversations and other distractions when you get within a certain distance of your ball.

- If your second shot will be an approach shot to the green, note where the pin placement is and the slope, if any, of the green. This will help determine where you want the ball to land and stop on the green.
- Study the yardage from where you are to where you want the ball to land. Most courses have markers of some kind at 250, 150 and 100 yards. The 150 yard marker may have a particular tree planted, or a stake, or a birdbox. Some use sprinkler heads in the fairway to mark yardage.
- Observe where the bunkers are placed and find a safe landing area. Focus on places—safe targets—to land the ball. Select the shot and the club. Start your pre-shot routine, being committed to the shot selected. If you become indecisive, most likely you will hit a poor shot. Confidence helps you stay with your first inclination.

### Strategy for Playing a Golf Hole

Decisions about how to play a hole require some understanding of the hole in terms of its strengths and weaknesses, then knowing your skills as a golfer and matching them to the hole. Playing a golf hole and the course is like planning a trip. You decide on a route to take and you develop plans in case a route is closed.

Strengths (difficulty) of a golf hole include: bunkers, water hazards, narrow landing areas in the fairway, fairway bunkers, tight pin placements, doglegs, small greens, lots of trees, high rough, and out of bounds. Weaknesses (easiness) of a golf hole include: wide fairways, large greens, no bunkers in front of the green, room behind the pins, and no out of bounds.

If you plan and select your route from the tee to the green carefully, you can avoid getting into situations that might create tough shots. Steps to take to keep the ball in play and avoid difficult situations include the following:

1. Know about your game, how far you hit each club on the average, which shots are your strengths and which your weaknesses. If you cannot hit with your driver, leave it in the car.
2. Learn the layout of the course. Study the scorecard, which usually has a diagram of each hole. Try to play with someone who knows the course. Figure 10.2 illustrates a sample scorecard with the course layout on the card. Most courses will have a diagram of the hole on the sign for that hole next to the tee.
3. Know the distance from the tee to any bunkers or water hazards. Determine the distance for safe landing areas in the fairway and use the club that you hit that far. If you know that a 5-wood will land in the water, use a little less club if you know you cannot hit over the water.
4. Learn how much you must get the ball to carry to go over a water hazard, bunker, or other situation. Many beginners typically do not hit enough club.
5. Choose carefully the target or landing area on a green. The location of the pin on the green can affect the club you choose. A pin placed near the back

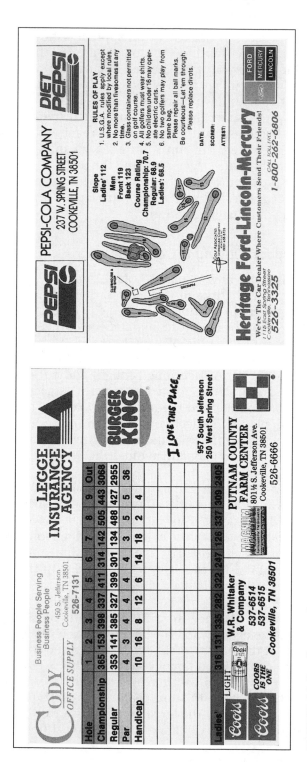

**FIGURE 10.2 Course Layout**

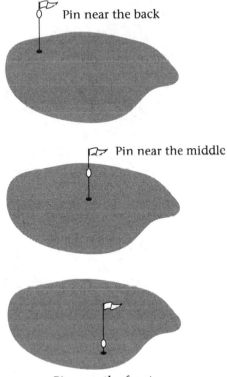

Pin near the back

Pin near the middle

Pin near the front

**FIGURE 10.3   Pin Placement Indicator**

of the green can add 10 to 20 more yards. The yardage markers give the distance from the marker to the center of the green on many courses. Some courses have pins with a marker on them. The marker looks like a buoy. When it is above the center of the flagstick, it means that the pin is past center; if below the middle, it means that the pin is in front of center; if in the middle, the pin is near the center of the green. Figure 10.3 gives an example of the pin placements.

6. Some greens may have out-of-bounds stakes behind them. Be sure to check for them. Always try to land the ball on the middle of the green if a pin is placed close to a bunker. If you try to go for the pin, you will most likely end up in the bunker with just a few feet on the green to make the next shot.

7. On a hole with a dogleg, you want to be sure to hit past the corner so that you will have a good approach shot to the green. Figure 10.4 illustrates the landing area for the hole with a dogleg in it.

8. Some holes have narrow landing areas for the tee shot. Use a club off the tee that will keep you in the fairway,

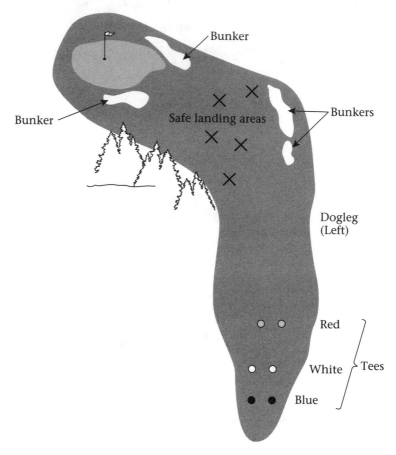

**FIGURE 10.4   Dogleg Hole.**   Safe Landing Areas

## Pre-shot Routine

The best thing to be said about a pre-shot routine is to develop one and use it, without exception, on every golf shot you make. It is designed to lock you in on the shot like radar. You are cluing your body that it is time to act. An essential of a pre-shot routine is to do the same thing before each shot. This repeatable procedure before each shot will help you relax, concentrate, and feel confident to execute each shot.

Golfers will develop an individual routine, but all should have key elements. These include the following basics: data gathering to select the shot; selecting the club; selecting the actual target and an intermediate target; visualizing the shot, feeling confident, and setting up to make the shot.

**Data Gathering.**   Go through the strategies described previously for gathering data as you approach your ball. This helps to determine the shot you want to make.

**Shot and Club Selection.**   Based on your calculations, determine the type of shot you want to make. This will depend on the lie of the ball, the wind conditions, knowing your abilities, the course strengths and weaknesses, and your strengths and weaknesses as a player. For example, you might be in heavy rough and have to use a sand wedge to hit, even though a sand wedge will not reach the green. Get the ball back into play so that your next shot will be easier to the green. Play smart.

**Target Selection.**   Select a terminal target or where you want the ball to land and stop. Determine an intermediate target a couple of feet in front of your ball in line with the final target.

**Visualizing the Shot and Feeling Confident.**   Picture the shot in your mind from a point behind the ball. See it just as you want it to look. Commit to making the shot. This will add to your confidence in making the shot. After seeing the shot you want, practice swing one or two times. This will help you "feel" the shot.

**Set-Up and Swing.**   From behind the ball, select an intermediate target. Align the clubface on the intermediate target. Align your feet and get into your posture. Look down the target line to check out the distance. Make the shot.

Each pre-shot routine differs from one person to another. All should include the elements described above. Figure 10.5 includes a Pre-shot Routine Skill Builder Checklist.

---

**Decision Making**

_____ examines lie of the ball
_____ determines distance to target
_____ determines which club is needed
_____ determines the landing area based on target selected (standing behind ball)
_____ identifies an intermediate target

**Set-Up**

_____ takes grip
_____ takes practice swing (from side of ball)
_____ aligns leading edge of clubface with intermediate target
_____ aligns right foot first, then left foot
_____ looks down target line
_____ uses a relaxation move, i.e. Waggle

**Comments:**

---

**FIGURE 10.5   Pre-shot Routine Skill Builder Checklist**

## Course Management Skill Builders

SELF-TALK DRILL

*Purpose:* To develop positive self-talk.

*Equipment:* iron or wood

*Activity:*

1. While practicing, while completing a skill-builder drill, or while playing, ask your partner to note every time you say or use negative statements directed to yourself. Write down the negative statements. Also note when you say something negative about yourself.
2. During your practice or play, set a goal to say at least ten positive statements about how you are doing. After each practice, drill, or play on the course, count the number of positive statements.

Goal = # of positive statements made per practice or playing session: _____ . Strive for at least ten statements.

POSITIVE PLANNING DRILL

*Purpose:* To develop positive thinking about hazards and special circumstances that arise during play.

*Formation:* partners sitting on practice range

*Activity:*

1. Your partner selects a situation; for example, you have landed in a bunker. Your partner asks you what you say about it. If you say a negative thought, say a positive thought. An example is: "I have so much trouble with sand shots. I am really in trouble now." Replace that thought with "If I relax and use my routine, I can make this shot."
2. Reverse roles. Your partner now is the player, and you select a difficult situation. Help your partner use positive thoughts and actions during the imagined situation.
3. Other situations are: landing in the rough, hitting out of bounds, having to make a shot near a water hazard.

Score = # of positive statements you were able to say for three different situations: _____

KNOW YOUR GAME DRILL

*Purpose:* To identify the strengths and weaknesses of your golf game.

*Equipment:* paper and pencil

*Activity:* For each skill listed, if it is a strength for you, place a plus by it. If it is a weakness, place a minus sign by it.

- _____ putting
- _____ chipping
- _____ pitching
- _____ tee shots
- _____ bunker shots
- _____ shots from the rough
- _____ fairway shots
- _____ shot pattern with each club/hook/slice
- _____ directional patterns/push/pull
- _____ concentration during play
- _____ tension control/ability to relax
- _____ temperament
- _____ self-talk
- _____ focus on safe landing areas

Score = # of strengths and weaknesses you are able to identify: _____

## ERRORS AND CORRECTIONS

*Error:* You focus on hazards or out of bounds areas when you are near these situations, saying to yourself, "Now, don't hit out of bounds."

*Correction:* Visualize the shot, landing in areas away from a hazard. Focus on what you want the ball to do.

*Error:* You have doubts about your ability to hit a particular shot during a round, such as having to chip from an uphill lie onto a green sloping downhill.

*Correction:* If you have practiced the shot, focus on the fact that you have and recall your successes.

*Error:* You have tee shots and fairway wood shots that tend to end up out of bounds or in the woods where you are left with difficult shots.

*Correction:* Select a more lofted wood for the tee shot. Instead of the driver, use a 3- or 5-wood. Apply the same strategy for fairway shots. Use a 5-wood instead of a 3-wood.

*Error:* On long par 4s and par 5s, you swing harder to try to get more distance, which usually results in a poor shot.

*Correction:* Relax and reduce the tension caused by a long hole. Swing in a relaxed manner and try to keep your tempo.

# 11

## PRACTICE, CONDITIONING, AND IMPROVING YOUR GAME

The practice of any motor skill, provided the practice is directed toward the correct movements involved, will lead to skill improvement. Most individuals do not devote enough time to practicing their golf game. When they do devote time, the practice session lacks organization. In many cases, what one sees is the novice purchasing a bucket of range balls, making a beeline to the range, pulling out a wood, and hitting away at one ball after another until the bucket is gone. So what was accomplished? Did the golfer go away feeling successful? How would one know if no goals were established and met? Practicing your golf game with a purpose is one of the most valuable investments of time you can make toward improving your game.

Although one does not have to be a top-notch athlete to play golf, some conditioning is helpful to your game and in preventing injuries. Developing a good exercise routine to help your game will keep you fit and playing golf for a lifetime. This chapter will provide the beginning golfer with strategies for developing and organizing a sound practice and conditioning routine.

### Learner Skills

1. Define different types of practice strategies and the purpose of each one.
2. Discuss methods of determining what aspects of your game need to be practiced and improved.
3. Develop a plan for practicing golf skills.
4. Develop a conditioning program for keeping fit to play golf.

### Prerequisite Skills

1. Understands and has experienced different skills such as chipping, pitching, putting, full swing, bunker shots, and play from the rough.
2. Experienced a playing lesson or has played at least one round of golf.
3. Recognizes basic ball flight errors.

## HOW TO PRACTICE

Before practicing, warm up your body by stretching. Focus on practice goals that were set for yourself. Keep making little changes until you feel satisfied that you reached your goals or outcomes. Take small breaks or rest periods rather than one long practice period. Fatigue can lead to more errors and lessen your focus. Indicate to yourself when you are being successful in accomplishing each practice goal. Leave your practice session with a good shot. Acknowledge it and allow yourself to enjoy what you accomplished.

## TYPES OF PRACTICE

One type of practice is related to getting ready to play a round of golf. This strategy is used just before playing. This is really a warm-up routine moreso than practice. You should develop a strategy for a good warm-up that will allow a few practice shots with most clubs.

A second type is practice that occurs after a round of golf is played. Most amateurs finish their round and head for the snack bar or parking lot. They rarely practice after they play. Yet, you will hear them say, "My putting was terrible," or "I couldn't hit a green to save my life." They would improve their game if they would practice right after a round.

A third type of practice is between rounds. For example, you may not play more than once a week or once every two weeks. In between these playing times, practice is important, particularly to keep a good tempo to your swing and to maintain some level of skill.

Another type of practice is during the winter when play may be very sporadic. There are many things a golfer can do during the off season to practice and keep skills sharp.

### Practice before Play or Warming Up

A key to practicing before a round is to arrive in plenty of time. Allow about 45 minutes to an hour for practicing before your tee time. The following strategies for practicing before play should allow you to warm up and get relaxed before you reach the first tee.

**Study the Course Layout.**    If you are playing at a new course, get a scorecard and study the layout. If the course has a lot of bunkers, you may want to practice sand shots or at least hit with your sand wedge at some point.

**Chipping.**    Head to the practice green with a small bucket of balls. Chip a few balls with your 8- and 7-irons. Be sure chipping is allowed on the practice green. Chip for 10 minutes.

**Putting**

- Putt for distance first, not at the holes. Putt from 30, 20, and 10 feet, trying to get the balls to roll the same distance. Putt five to seven balls to three or four holes. Start with longer distances, trying to lag the balls close and then one-putt the balls into the holes.
- Putt from shorter distances of 10 feet, 5 feet, and 3 feet. Try to create a smooth stroke. Putt for about 20 minutes.

**Bunker Practice.**    If a practice bunker is available, hit shots for different distances using your sand and pitching wedges. Get a feel for the sand. If the course has few or no bunkers, eliminate this step and devote more time to putting. Hit sand shots for 5 minutes.

**Range.**    Go to the range and stretch your back muscles. Do some trunk twists, toe touching, and swing two clubs slowly. Start with short irons, hitting odd- or even-numbered clubs. Hit about five balls with each club. Actually visualize the first tee and what kind of shot you want to make. Hit with the club you plan to use on the first tee. Be sure to go through a good pre-shot routine each time you hit. Make full-swing shots on the range for 10 or 15 minutes.

**Mental Activity.**    Go to a spot near the first tee and relax. Breathe deeply and focus on the first hole. Visualize your first shot heading down the fairway. Think key thoughts such as I plan to play well today, I will use a good pre-shot routine. Mentally rehearse for 2 or 3 minutes.

## Practice after Play

Practice after a round may be the most productive type of practice for improving your game. The errors and things you did well should be fresh in your mind. It is particularly important to analyze how you played if you wish to practice after the round. Analyzing your round will help you establish priorities and goals for practice following play. Figure 11.1, the Beginner's Round Summary Log, provides a grid for analyzing your play during a round in a simplified manner.

| Hole | Par | Score | No. of shots from tee to green | Fairways hit from tee/club use | Shot flight patterns R. L. S* | No. of putts | Attention G. P** | Chip shots C. L. S*** | Pitch shots C. L. S |
|------|-----|-------|--------------------------------|--------------------------------|-------------------------------|--------------|------------------|-----------------------|---------------------|
| 1 | | | | | | | | | |
| 2 | | | | | | | | | |
| 3 | | | | | | | | | |
| 4 | | | | | | | | | |
| 5 | | | | | | | | | |
| 6 | | | | | | | | | |
| 7 | | | | | | | | | |
| 8 | | | | | | | | | |
| 9 | | | | | | | | | |
| 10 | | | | | | | | | |
| 11 | | | | | | | | | |
| 12 | | | | | | | | | |
| 13 | | | | | | | | | |
| 14 | | | | | | | | | |
| 15 | | | | | | | | | |
| 16 | | | | | | | | | |
| 17 | | | | | | | | | |
| 18 | | | | | | | | | |

*Right, left, straight     **Good, poor     ***Close, long, short

**FIGURE 11.1   Beginner's Round Summary Log**

The log is divided into the long game (tee shots into fairways, greens hit in regulation), the short game (chipping, pitching, putting), attention/distractions, and ball flight. By noting each of these aspects of play from your round, you should have a good idea about what parts of your golf game need to be addressed during a post-play practice session. Make the following notations related to the skills listed above.

## Long Game

Your long game notations should focus on the number of tee shots that landed safely and the number of greens reached in regulation, Keep in mind which club such as a 3-wood or driver, brought the most success from the tee.

Indicate shot characteristics, such as pulls, pushes, slices, hooks or shots that were off target. You may find that you slice your driver and that there are usually hazards available for a big slice.

## Short Game

For the short game, note chip and pitch shot characteristics, such as the number made out of the total; the shot characteristics, such as fat, thin, or topped; and the ball's flight patterns. Putting notations should include the number of putts for the total holes played, the number of three-putts, and ball roll characteristics such as pushes, pulls, and those left short or long more than 2 feet.

## Mental Aspects/Attention

Note the number of times you used a good pre-shot routine and really concentrated on shots. Indicate your self-talk outcomes—how you played after negative and positive statements made about yourself or your game. Think about the situations that made you tense, such as being in a hazard.

Think about how well you were able to control your temper and what circumstances, if any, brought about changes in your mood while playing. For example, if you know that slow play makes you angry, develop strategies to eliminate this response.

Review your log and prioritize what aspects of your game need improving. Plan a practice strategy around the identified areas. A practice plan should include the following aspects.

1. Identify practice needs. Examples include: three-putted on nine greens and pulled putts, shots were off target to the left, topped shots, seemed to be tense during the swing.
2. Establish goals for the practice session. Examples include: improve alignment, as shots were off target; reduce three-putts by practicing lag putting or alignment.
3. Decide on a practice strategy. Establish criteria for your practice results. For instance, if your long putts stopped way short of the hole and were mostly pulled, a strategy would be to review alignment and swing path. Practice swing-path drills and putt for distances of 15 and 20 feet. You might set a goal of lagging seven out of ten balls to within 2 feet or less from the hole from a distance of 15 to 20 feet.

Practice session _____        Date _____Time allotted _____

Skills to be practiced:


Goal/s:



Skill Builder drills:




Equipment:



Evaluation:



# of goals met _____

Suggestions for next practice:



**FIGURE 11.2   Practice Strategy Log**


Figure 11.2 provides an example of a Practice Strategy Log. You can use the log to plan an effective and productive practice session. Simply identify what needs to be practiced, set a goal, identify a strategy, and practice away. Monitor the results of the practice session by recording your progress.

### Practice between Rounds

You must decide how much time you have to devote to practice between rounds. Practice whenever you are able to work it into your schedule. Short, distributed practice sessions are more productive than long, tiring ones. Twenty-minute sessions scattered throughout the week may be more productive than one long session of 2 hours or more.

Practice does not always occur at a golf course or range. There are many opportunities to practice in your home or yard. When you are at home, try these strategies.

Read a magazine or instruction book about golf that addresses your areas in need of improvement. Watch a golf video that addresses your needs. These may be rented from video stores or library loan. Watch a tournament on a weekend and note how deliberately players go through a pre-shot routine or how much tempo is in their swing. Swing a club slowly in front of a mirror, trying to include key positions in the swing. Practice gripping as you watch television or putt on the carpet.

Practice chipping into an open umbrella in the yard. The following example will give you an idea of how to practice your game throughout the week in short segments. The activities include conditioning as well.

### Monday through Wednesday

Work on conditioning, including strengthening, stretching, and cardiovascular activities such as walking, cycling, or low-impact aerobics.

Monday: Putt on carpet, working on distance control.

Tuesday: For 15 minutes, swing clubs in front of mirror and work on grip, stance, and posture.

Wednesday: Read a golf magazine just before bedtime. Watch a golf video.

### Thursday through Sunday

Thursday: Go to the range and practice alignment, hitting balls to targets for 20 minutes. Work on chipping and putting on the practice green for 45 minutes.

Friday: Work at home on putting in the morning and chipping in the evening for 20 or 30 minutes.

Saturday: Practice for 30 to 45 minutes before playing. Play eighteen holes, indicating in your log good aspects of your game and those needing improvement.

Sunday: Watch a golf tournament on television. Attend a golf tournament, final round, if one is in your area.

### Off-Season Practice

During the winter, when play is reduced or not possible unless you are the heartiest of souls, practice can still continue. Practice can be similar to the weekly activities described above. Stress the short-game skills in the winter as well as a conditioning program.

## PRACTICE POINTS

Practice can become boring on occasion and seem like a chore. You can avoid becoming bored by doing several things. Practice as if you were playing a round, creating situations and trying to solve them on the range. Practice with someone, creating putting or chipping contests.

Practice making small gains as mentioned in the skill builder drills. A partner will be able to observe you, using a Skill Builder Checklist, and provide feedback related to your execution of the skill. Be patient when you practice. You may have reached a plateau in skill development. It may be awhile before you see any great leaps in improvement. If you are making a change in your swing as a result of a lesson, again, be patient. It is hard to change old habits and learn new ones. It may take up to three weeks to see consistent improvement in changes that you are making. Try to practice as you would play golf.

### Establish a Personal Par

Beginning golfers will not shoot par golf. Even professionals and collegiate amateurs do not always shoot par. Set your own par for each hole. Simply get a scorecard and write your own par for each hole. You may decide that you will be able to par at least one hole on the front and one hole on the back. The other holes may have bogeys and one or two double bogeys as par. Once you reach your personal goals for par, establish new ones, changing double bogeys to bogeys and adding one or two more pars per round.

### What Should I Practice the Most?

Work on the weakest parts of your game the most. However, the short game—putting, chipping, and pitching—is used more often than any other shots in golf. Spend sufficient time or at least two-thirds to three-fourths of it on the short game.

### Acknowledge Success

Do not forget to reward yourself for doing things correctly. When you practice or practice/play, say good things to yourself, such as "That was a good putt," "I landed in the fairway, great tee shot."

## CONDITIONING FOR PLAY

Investing time in physical conditioning will add to your golf game and help prevent injuries, especially to your back. Flexibility and strength in the big muscles of the body contribute to how far you are able to hit a golf ball. Some instructors will insist that the left side of the body is involved more in the swing than the right side, but both sides of the body are used and should be balanced in terms of conditioning. Loss of strength and stretchability of the muscles reduces the power of the swing, particularly as one gets older.

You do not have to exercise every day; three times a week is sufficient, particularly for strengthening. Stretching should be done nearly every day and can be easily worked into your daily routine. For example, do stretches when you finish your shower or just before you go to bed. There are a few guidelines you should follow before and during your conditioning program.

## *Flexibility/Stretching*

1. Always consult a physician before beginning a conditioning program, particularly if you have a health problem or condition.
2. Always warm up gently before you begin strengthening or flexibility exercises. Walk quickly or jog in place for 5 minutes.
3. Avoid bouncing to stretch. Use a slow, bending motion and hold the position for 10 seconds. Stretch until you feel a tug, but not a pain, at the muscles. If you are hurting, you have stretched too far.
4. Gradually increase the range or distance stretched.

## *Strengthening/Endurance*

1. Always warm up your muscles before lifting weights. Use similar warm-up activities as for stretching.
2. Begin lifting with the number of pounds you can comfortably move. Do lifts in sets of eight or ten repetitions. Gradually increase to three sets of ten repetitions and add more weight cautiously. You want to avoid injury to joints and connective tissue, such as ligaments and tendons.
3. For endurance, try any type of low-impact aerobic activity, such as walking as you play golf, cycling, swimming, or rope jumping. This will add strength to your legs and total body. Figures 11.3 through 11.8 illustrate basic conditioning exercises to help your game.

Figures 11.3 through 11.4 illustrate examples of flexibility exercises. Figures 11.5 through 11.8 illustrate examples of upper-body strengthening exercises. You should walk, cycle, or stair climb or combine these with swimming to improve lower body strength.

**FIGURE 11.3A    Trunk Rotator Flexibility**

**FIGURE 11.3B    Trunk Rotator Flexibility**

**FIGURE 11.4A    Hamstring and Calf Stretch Flexibility**

**FIGURE 11.4B    Hamstring and Calf Stretch Flexibility**

**FIGURE 11.5A** Abdominal Curls/Rotation Strength

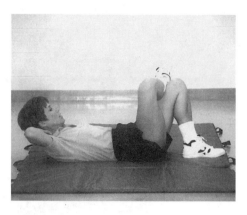

**FIGURE 11.5B** Abdominal Curls/Rotation Strength

**FIGURE 11.6A** Sidearm Lifts Strength

**FIGURE 11.6B** Sidearm Lifts Strength

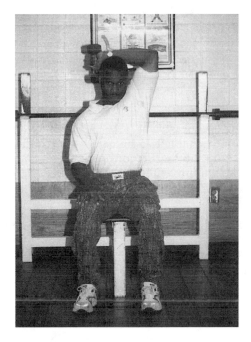

**FIGURE 11.7A** Triceps Extension
Strength

**FIGURE 11.7B** Triceps Extension
Strength

**FIGURE 11.8A** Arm Curls Front
Strength

**FIGURE 11.8B** Arm Curls Front
Strength

**Practice Skill Builders**

ERROR IDENTIFICATION DRILL

*Purpose:* To identify aspects of play that need improvement.

*Equipment:* paper and pencils

*Activity:* Review your practice session or play of at least four holes. Write at least three aspects of play that need improvement. Examples: pulled 75 percent of putts; did not use pre-shot routine on 25 percent of shots; left chip shots either long or short to make an easy putt to get up and down. Write a goal for each improvement need identified. An example is:

*Goal 1*
  Using an 8- and 9-iron from 10 yards from the hole, chip seven out of ten shots so they land within 3 feet of the hole.
  Identify a drill or strategy for meeting the goals stated.

*Goal 1*
Strategies:   _Review chipping strategies. Chip for distance._

_Chip to 5-foot circle and 3-foot circle._

Completion date: _____

  Try writing a goal that relates to a need for improvement in your golf game. Include the skill, the conditions, and desired outcome. Refer to the example above.

*Your goal:* _____

_____

*Strategies:* _____

_____

Completion date: _____

COMMON ERRORS DURING PLAY

*Error:* Shots go fairly straight but are off target, pushed or pulled.

*Correction:* Check alignment: Alignment may be to the left or right of the target. Check the distance from the ball; the distance may be too far. Check the swing path; the club shaft may be crossing the target line, causing the path to be inside out or outside in.

*Error:* Shots are left short of the target but have reasonable flight patterns.

*Correction:* Use one less club. You may be under-clubbing distances.

*Error:* Balls are topped or hit thin.

*Correction:* Check to see that the club is not held deeply in right palm (left palm for left-handers). The ball should be positioned near center or just front of center. A ball placed too far forward can cause topping. Check for maintaining posture throughout the swing.

*Error:* When confronted with hazards, you often land your ball in them.

*Correction:* Use a good pre-shot routine, focusing on a safe target instead of the hazard; and visualize the shot you want to make. Choose a club that will leave you short of the hazard.

*Error:* When playing, you have a lot of tension.

*Correction:* Take deep breaths, tense your muscles for 10 seconds, then relax. Visualize one of your best golf shots. Take relaxed practice swings.

*Error:* You focus on bad shots or think about the last two holes and how difficult they can be.

*Correction:* Think about the present shot only; put other thoughts aside; concentrate on a good pre-shot routine; focus on the positive aspects of your playing ability.

# APPENDIX A

# ETIQUETTE

## RESPECT FELLOW PLAYERS

- Be quiet when next or near players preparing to swing.
- Stand to the side and not too close to someone preparing to swing.
- Stay off a player's line of putt on the green.
- Warn other players of an approaching shot by yelling "Fore."
- Compliment others on a good shot and ignore a bad one.
- Avoid loud outbursts or club throwing.
- Record your score for a hole after leaving the putting green.
- Check periodically to see if groups behind you are having to wait.

## PLAY QUICKLY AND EFFICIENTLY

- Be ready to hit when it is your turn; know the club you need and the distance.
- Make one practice swing.
- Keep pace with the group in front; if a hole is open in front, your pace is too slow.
- Help others in your group to look for their balls.
- Never look for a ball for more than 5 minutes.
- Let faster groups play through.
- Wait until players are well out of range before hitting. If your view is obstructed, be sure to check that no other players are in range.

## *LEAVE THE COURSE BETTER THAN YOU FOUND IT*

- Drive on the cart paths and follow the cart rule of the day. Be sure to check in the pro shop or with the starter.
- Drive in a reasonable and safe manner and from the driver's side of the cart.
- Sit well into the cart; avoid leaning outside or sitting on the edge of the seat.
- Children under 14 should not be allowed to drive the carts.
- Leave the cart near the exit side of the green when your group gets out to putt.
- Leave the cart 30 to 40 feet from the green.
- Obey all cart signs and instructions or requests from the course staff.
- Pull carts should be left well off the green and tees (10 feet away is a good practice).
- Rake the bunker after you have made your shot.
- Keep litter in trash containers and pick it up if you see it in your path.
- Be careful not to bend or break tree limbs or shrubs; it is against the rules.
- Replace all divots.
- Repair ball marks on the green. Repair an extra ball mark if no group is waiting to hit.
- Report anyone damaging the course or golf carts.

# APPENDIX B

# TECHNIQUES FOR ERROR CORRECTION

| Error | Corrective Measures |
|---|---|
| Ball Flight—Slice | Check for open clubface at impact and weak grip—hands are usually way ahead of clubhead at impact. Note hand position on forwardswing—right palm is facing skyward for slice instead of the right wrist rotating over the left (back of left hand should be in a handshake position and toe of the club pointing skyward). An open stance will also contribute to the slice.<br>Make one or two changes at a time. Correct grip first. Practice the correct wrist and hand positions at impact and on the forwardswing. Practice correct set-up positions. |
| Ball Flight—Hook | Check for a strong grip, closed clubface at impact, and early excessive wrist rotation in the forwardswing. At waist high on the backswing, the left hand will be more palm up instead of in the handshake position with toe of the clubhead pointing skyward. Toe of the club will point at 10 o'clock on an imaginary clock face rather than the desired 12 o'clock position (toe of the clubhead points to sky). A closed stance also contributes to the hook.<br>Correct the strong grip. Stress practice of the hand and club positions at impact and on the forwardswing. Stress the correct club position at waist high on the backswing. The wrist should be flat at the top of the backswing and not bowed. Practice a square impact position and good, square set-up position. |
| Ball Flight—Pull | Check for a good body turn on the backswing. A poor turn can result in an outside to inside approach to the ball, causing it to fly left. Also, the clubface may be square or pointing left. Overuse of the upper body and right shoulder in the downswing can cause pulled shots.<br>Correct by making sure there is a good upper body turn away from the target. Feel the back toward the target at the top of the backswing. Emphasize using the lower body more on the downswing rather than over-leading with the upper body, particularly the right shoulder and arm. |

| | |
|---|---|
| Ball Flight—Push | Check that the club is taken to parallel to target line at the half backswing position. Taking the club too far inside by over-turning the upper body results in an inside to outside club path. The clubface will be square to this line. The swing resembles more of a baseball swing (flat and round). Over-rotating the hips toward the target too early can cause the club to move inside to outside. The club should be parallel at the top and not point to right of the target.<br>Correct by practicing a good take-away and check for a parallel club to target line at halfway back and at the top. Practice the correct club positions at halfway back, at the correct downswing move, and at impact position. Stress timing of upper and lower body. |
| Fat Shot | This is the result of the club contacting the ground before the ball. Check for the correct ball position in relation to the stance. The ball should be at the center or just forward. Also, failure to transfer the body's weight to the left side contributes to this shot.<br>Correct by producing a good set-up, keeping posture consistent throughout the swing. Practice a good weight shift to the left side and good follow-through. |
| Thin or Topped Shot | The clubface is contacting the ball at the equator or above it. This results in a low rolling ball. Check for a consistent spine angle throughout the swing and good posture at set-up, particularly the head; it should not be buried in the chest. The arms should be extended at impact. Too much bend in the left arm can cause these shots. Check the ball's position; it may be too far forward in the stance.<br>Correct by making a proper set-up to the ball. Practice a good swing motion without trying to consciously hit the ball. Practice good extension at impact and on the forwardswing. Practice clipping tees from the turf until consistent contact with the ground occurs. |
| Skying | The ball is impacted with woods at the top of the clubface. A ball position that is rear of center assists with this shot. An open stance can contribute to the problem as well. The hands are well ahead of the clubhead at impact, and the body's weight is too far to the left side. This makes the clubhead descend at a steep angle into the ball, causing it to fly high with reduced distance for the wood being used.<br>Correct by establishing the correct ball position for woods, just forward of center and inside the left heel for a driver. The impact position should be stressed (hands should not be ahead of the clubhead). Be sure the wrists and hands begin their rotation in the forwardswing. |
| Shanking | The ball has been contacted with the hosel or curved part of the neck of the iron club. The ball shoots to the right. Check for an extremely open clubface at impact. Also leading with the right shoulder in the downswing contributes to this shot. Check the downswing position of the hands. If the left knuckles are pointing more skyward, the club will come in too shallow to the ball, causing it to hit on the hosel. The outside to inside swing path and holding the weight back on the right side contribute to this shot.<br>Correct the swing path, making sure the hands are not over-turning on the backswing, throwing the clubface wide open. Practice the correct club and hand positions at halfway back (toe pointing skyward and left hand in the handshake position) Be sure weight is returned to the left side on downswing and follow through. |

# APPENDIX C

# GOLF RESOURCES

## Videos

*Gary Player on Golf.* The Master Source Video.

*Golf Digest's Learning Library.* Golf Digest Video Center, Trumbull, CT, 06611–0395. 5520 Park Ave. Box 395, Trumbull CT, 06611. Vol. 1 A Swing For A Lifetime, Vol. 2 Find Your Own Fundamentals, Vol. 3 Driving For Accuracy, Vol. 4 Sharpen Your Short Irons, Vol. 5 Saving Par From The Sand, Vol. 6 Putting For Profit, Vol. 7 When The Chips Are Down, Vol. 8 Winning Pitch Shots, Vol. 9 Hitting Long Shots, Vol. 10 Trouble Shots: Great Escapes.

*60 Yards and In with Raymond Floyd.* Ohlmeyer Communications Company, Los Angeles, CA.

*Golf Lessons From Sam Snead.* Star Video Productions: 10701 Wilshire Blvd. Suite 2001, Los Angeles, CA, 90024.

*Golf My Way, Jack Nicklaus.* World Vision Home Video, Taft Broadcasting Company.

*Golf The Miller Way.* Johnny Miller. Morris Video, 2730 Monterey #105 Torrance, CA, 90503

*How To Win And Win Again.* Curtis Strange. Home Video Inc.

*Ken Venturi's Better Golf Now.* HPG Home Video, Union Station, 400 S. Houston, Suite 230, Dallas, TX 75202

*Ken Venturi's Encyclopedia of Golf.* Master Grip, 2450 Turquoise Cir. P. O. Box 2555, Newbury Park, CA 91320

*Scramble To Better Golf.* Fuzzy Zoeller. Video Magazine International, 22 Church St., Liberty Corner, NJ 07938

*The Art of Putting.* Ben Crenshaw. HPG Home Video, Union Station, 400 S. Houston, Suite 230, Dallas, TX, 75202

*The Azinger Way.* Paul Azinger. International Sport Videos, 302 S. Massachusetts Ave., Lakeland, FL, 33801

*The Best Of Trevino's Golf Tips.* Lee Trevino. Lee Trevino Enterprises, 10333 Ashton Ave., Los Angeles, CA, 90024

*The Etiquette Of Golf: Moving The Game Along.* Heather Productions, 68 Mayfair Dr., Pittsburgh, PA, 15228

*The Official Rules Of Golf.* Explained by Tom Watson and Peter Alliss. Caravatt Instructional Video, 49 Riverside Ave. Westport, CT, 06880

## CD ROMs and Computer Software

### Instruction

*Golf Tips: Breaking 100: With David Ledbetter.* Diamar Interactive Corporation, 600 University St., Seattle, WA 98101. 206/340–5975, @ $49.00

*Golf Tips: Breaking 90 (See above address)* @ $49.00

*ESPN Interactive Golf: Lower your score with Tom Kite.* Intellimedia Sports, Inc., Suite 300, Two Piedmont Center, Atlanta, GA 30305. 1–800/269–2101, @ $49.00

## Game Play

*Microsoft Golf 2.0.* Microsoft, $49.00

*Links Pro MacIntosh.* Access Software, $49.95

*Picture Perfect Golf.* Lyriq, $79.95

## Golf Information

*Online Golf–America On Line.* Link up with golfers worldwide, review travel information and the Pro Tour. Type the keyword: iGOLF

*World Wide Web.* Type: rec.sport.golf. or http://www.golf.com.

*America's Great Golf Resorts.* Plan golf trips to some of the greatest courses in America. Treasure House Publishing, Inc. 202/881–6461, @ $37.00

# GLOSSARY

**Ace**   A hole in one.

**Addressing the ball**   Taking the stance and grounding the club, except in a hazard, before taking a swing.

**Approach shot**   A stroke played with the intent of landing it on the putting surface.

**Apron**   The short, grassy area immediately surrounding the putting area.

**Away**   The ball farther from the hole shall be played first.

**Backspin**   A backward spinning of the ball caused by hitting down on the ball. This is used to stop the ball quickly as it lands on the green.

**Backswing**   The portion of the swing that moves the club away from the ball and ends when moving the club downward toward the ball.

**Ball mark**   Any indention made in the putting surface caused by the ball landing on it.

**Back nine**   The last nine holes of an eighteen-hole golf course, also referred to as "in" on the score card.

**Birdie**   A scoring term indicating one stroke under par on a hole.

**Bogey**   A scoring term indicating one stroke over par on a hole.

**Break**   The curved line the ball will roll because of the slope of the fairway or green, wind, or grass grain on the green.

**Bunker**   A hazard made of a sandy or grassy depression designed to form an obstacle on the course. Grassy areas in a sand bunker are not considered part of the bunker. (Note that "sand trap" is a term not used in the rule book.)

**Casual water**   A temporary accumulation or freestanding water, not considered a hazard or part of the course. Dew is not considered casual water. Player is entitled to a drop without penalty if it interferes with stance or swing.

**Course rating**   A number used to indicate the playing difficulty of a course for scratch golfers.

**Chip shot**   A shot designed to send the ball to the green with a low trajectory. The ball has more ground time than air time.

**Chunk**   A mishit, striking the ground before the ball, resulting in poor ball contact or a fat shot.

**Closed clubface**   The toe of the club leads the heel, making the leading edge of the clubface less than 90 degrees to the target line or pointing left of the intended flight line.

**Closed stance**   A stance in which the right foot is back from the stance line, making the distance between the target and stance lines wider at the rear portion of the two lines rather than parallel.

**Clubface**   The hitting surface of the club head.

**Clubhead**   The part of the club designed to hit the ball.

**Cup**   The container in the hole on the putting surface. This term is also used to refer to the hole.

**Divot**   A piece of turf cut from the fairway when making a stroke. All divots should be replaced after making the shot.

**Dogleg**   A hole on the course in which the fairway curves to the right or left.

**Double bogey**   A term used to describe a score of two over par for a given hole.

**Draw**   A shot that curves slightly from right to left in flight.

**Drive**   A shot played from the tee with the driver.

**Driver**   A 1-wood used primarily to execute tee shots.

**Duck hook**   A shot which travels low and sharply to the left more than a hook shot. It is also called a snap hook.

**Duffer**   The name for a poor player.

**Eagle**   A score of two under par on a hole.

**Explosion shot**   A sand shot made when the ball has a buried lie in a bunker. The club makes a sharp descending blow, displacing a large amount of sand.

**Fade**   A shot that curves slightly from left to right in flight. A fade has the opposite ball fight from a draw.

**Fairway**   The short-mowed area of ground between the tee and the green.

**Fat shot**   A shot in which the clubhead strikes the ground before it hits the ball, usually caused by late shifting of the weight to the left side or lowering the upper body substantially on the downswing.

**Flagstick**   The marker that indicates the location of the hole on the green.

**Follow-through**   The completion of the swing.

**Fore**   The warning cry in golf to let anyone know there is danger of being struck from a hit ball.

**Foursome**   A group of four players. Golf is typically played in foursomes on busy courses. It is also a type of match in which two players play two others.

**Fringe**   The closely mowed grass, cut shorter than the fairway, which surrounds the green. Another name for the fringe is the apron.

**Front nine**   The first nine holes of an eighteen-hole course. Also referred to as "out" on the scorecard.

**Getting up and down**   Making a shot from off of the green and sinking or one-putting.

**Green**   The surface prepared for putting, containing the hole and flagstick.

**Green fee**   The amount charged a golfer for use of the golf course.

**Grip**   Taking hold of the club, or the position of the hands on the club. It is also the part of the club with a leather or rubber material indicating the portion of the club to be held.

**Gross score**   The actual score of a hole or a round before handicap strokes are deducted.

**Handicap**   The number indicating a golfer's scoring ability. It is determined, in simple terms, by taking 85 percent of the difference between a predetermined course rating and a player's average score on five or more rounds. It is an equalizing system that allows golfers to complete on equal terms with each other.

**Hazard**   A term used in USGA Rules to indicate a sand or water areas.

**Heel of the club**   The part of the clubhead nearest the golfer or opposite the toe of the clubhead.

**Hole**   The receptacle on the green, 4 1/4 inches in diameter and at least 4 inches deep. It is also used to describe each division on the course.

**Hole out**   Putting the ball into the cup to complete the play of a hole.

**Honor**   The right to tee off first on a hole as a result of having the lowest score on the preceding hole or winning the coin toss on the first tee.

**Hook**   A shot that curves from right to left as a result of counter-clockwise spin on the ball from a closed clubface at impact.

**Intermediate target**   A point on the ground about a foot in front of the ball in line with the target; used to help in alignment.

**Intended line of flight**   The imaginary line that runs through the ball, extending forward on a line on which the player wants the ball to travel

**Irons**   The clubs numbered 1 through 9, pitching wedge, and sand wedge, which generally come in a matched set.

**Hosel**   The part of the clubhead into which the shaft fits.

**Lag**   A long-length putt that stops close enough to the hole, leaving an easy putt.

**Lateral water hazard**   A water hazard that runs parallel to the fairway and is marked by red stakes.

**Lie**   The position of the ball at rest. Also, the angle of the clubhead in relation to the shaft.

**Links**   A term used to describe golf courses adjacent to the sea or ocean; e.g., The Links at Key Biscayne.

**Lip out**   A putt that rolls around the cup but stays out.

**Lob**   A shot hit with a wedge with a great deal of loft, which lands softly.

**Loft**   The angle of pitch on a clubface; also refers to the flight of the ball.

**Loose impediments**   Twigs, pinecones, rocks, leaves, worms, etc., which are not fixed.

**LPGA**   Ladies Professional Golf Association.

**Match play**   A form of competition played by winning the most holes. The person making the lowest score on a hole wins the hole.

**Medal play**   A form of competition based on the lowest score for a round. Also referred to as stroke play.

**Metal woods**   Clubs referred to as "woods" that are actually constructed of a metal such as stainless steel. Some are constructed of graphite.

**Mulligan**   An illegal practice of taking a second shot from the first tee if the first shot was poor. A mulligan is not recognized by the Rules of Golf.

**Net score**   The score for a hole or a round after the handicap strokes are subtracted.

**Obstruction**   Any artificial object erected, placed, or abandoned on the course. Tractors, posts, utility boxes, hoses, rakes are obstructions.

**On the dance floor**   To be on the green.

**Open stance**   The left foot and left side of the body are away from the parallel stance line.

**Out of bounds**   Any area of the course outside of the designated markers, usually fences or white stakes. A ball may not be played if it is out of bounds. The shot must be replayed from the original spot of the shot.

**Par**   The scoring standard on a hole, determined by the hole's length and allowing two putts on the green.

**Penalty stroke**   A stroke added to the score as a result of a rule violation.

**Pitch shot**   A shot that produces high trajectory and little roll on the ball, primarily used as an approach shot onto the green.

**PGA**   Professional Golfers' Association

**Play through**   Allowing a faster group behind a slower group to pass them. The slower group signals the group behind by waving an arm to motion them forward if it is safe for them to proceed.

**Provisional ball**   A legal second ball played when the first ball is thought to be out of bounds or lost outside a hazard. The player must declare that a provisional ball is being played before hitting it.

**Pull**   A shot that travels in a straight line of flight but to the left of the intended target.

**Push**   A shot that travels in a straight line of flight but to the right of the intended target.

**Putt**   A stroke played on the green with the intent of hitting the ball into the cup.

**Putter**   A flat-bladed club designed for making a stroke on the green.

**Reading the green**   The attempt to determine the path and speed on which the ball should roll to a hole on the green.

**Relief**   Legal permission to move the ball away from trouble on the course without penalty.

**Rough**  Higher grass and other vegetation bordering the fairway. The rough is less manicured than the fairway.

**Scratch golfer**  A player who has a zero handicap and generally scores par on the holes.

**Scratch play**  The form of play or competition in which no handicap strokes are given.

**Set-up**  Preparing to swing, which includes the grip, stance, posture, and alignment of the body. Also called the address.

**Short game**  The shots played from around the green and on the green, referred to as chip and pitch shots, greenside bunker shots and putting.

**Sky**  This refers to a shot trajectory that flies higher and shorter than normal for the club being used. It is caused by a steep approach to the ball and hitting too far under the ball with less than solid contact.

**Slice**  A shot that curves to the right in flight as a result of clockwise spin on the ball from an open clubface at impact.

**Sole**  The bottom of the clubhead; also refers to resting the clubhead on the ground, or grounding the club.

**Square clubface**  The clubface is aligned at a 90-degree angle to the target line (perpendicular). This produces a straight flight on the ball.

**Square stance**  The feet and body are parallel to the target line.

**Stance**  The position of the player's feet when setting up to hit the ball.

**Stroke**  The forward movement of the club with the intention of striking the ball.

**Take-away**  This is the initial move away from the ball to start the backswing.

**Tap in**  A short, easy putt.

**Target line**  The intended line of flight of the golf ball or an imaginary straight line between the ball and the target.

**Tee**  A peg on which the ball is placed before striking it from the teeing area. Also refers to the beginning point for each hole on the course, also called teeing area.

**Tee markers**  Markers placed on the tee to indicate the forward limits of the teeing area.

**Tee time**  The designated time to begin the play of a round. This may be requested or assigned by a starter at a course.

**Tempo**  Refers to the pace of a golfer's swing.

**Through the green**  The whole of the course, except the teeing ground and putting green of the hole being played, and all hazards.

**Toe**  The outer edge of the clubhead farthest from the shaft and golfer at address.

**Tend the flag**  A request made by a fellow player to remove the flagstick after the ball has been struck.

**Topped shot**  A stroke that hits the ball near the top causing it to roll along the ground.

**Up and down**   To hole out in two strokes from off the green.

**Unplayable lie**   Anywhere on the course except in a water hazard where players may declare that they are unable to play their ball. This results in a one-stroke penalty.

**Victory lap**   Refers to a ball that rolls around the lip or edge of the cup and then falls in.

**Water hazard**   Any lake, sea, pond, or stream that runs across the fairway; indicated by yellow stakes.

**Whiff**   An intentional swing at the ball that completely misses it.

**Winter rules**   Local rules established to protect the fairway of a course and which allow improvement of the lie of the ball. The lie may be improved either a grip length on the club or a club length no closer to the hole. Also used in the winter months when course fairways may not be in the best playing shape.

# BIBLIOGRAPHY

Alcott, A., and Wade, D. 1991. *Amy Alcott's guide to women's golf.* New York: The Penguin Group.

Anderson, J. M. 1992. *Winning golf made easy.* New York: Sterling Publishing Co.

Ballard, J. 1981. *How to perfect your golf swing: Using connection and the seven common denominators.* Trumbull, CT: Golf Digest Books.

Blanchard, K. 1992. *Playing the great game of golf: Making every minute count.* New York: William Morrow and Company.

Chamberlain, P. 1985. *Winning Golf.* New York: Sterling Publishing Co.

Gallaway, T. 1981. *The inner game of golf.* New York: Random House.

Hoeger, W. K., and Hoeger, S. A. 1993. *Fitness and Wellness.* Englewood, Colo. Morton Publishing Co.

Hogan, C. 1993. Learning golf: The how-to-learn book for aspiring golfers. Sedona, AZ: Sports Enhancement Associates.

Keogh, B. K., and Smith, C. E. 1985. *Personal par: A psychological system of golf for women.* Champaign, Ill.: Human Kinetics.

Kite, T., and Dennis, L. 1990. *How to play consistent golf.* Trumbull, CT: Golf Digest/Tennis, Inc. and New York: Pocket Books.

Kostis, P., and Dennis, L. 1982. *The inside path to better golf.* Trumbull, CT: Golf Digest/Tennis, Inc.

Leadbetter, D. 1990. *The golf swing.* Lexington, Mass.: The Stephen Greene Press.

Leadbetter, D. 1993. *David Leadbetter's faults and fixes.* New York: Harper Collins.

Lopez, N., and Wade, D. 1987. *Nancy Lopez's: The complete golfer.* New York: Contemporary Books.

Lupo, M. V., and Lupo, D. 1992. *How to master a great golf swing.* Chicago: Contemporary Books.

McLean, J., and Dennis, L. 1990. *Golf Digest's book of drills.* Trumbull, CT: Golf Digest Books.

Nicklaus, J., and Bowden, K. 1974. *Golf my way.* New York: Simon and Schuster.

Nicklaus, J. 1984. *The full swing.* Trumbull, CT: Golf Digest/Tennis, Inc.

Penick, H. 1993. *Harvey Penick's little red book.* New York: Simon and Schuster.

Toski, B., and Flick, J. 1978. *How to become a complete golfer.* New York: Simon and Schuster.

Watson, T., and Hannigan, F. 1992. *The rules of golf*. Trumbull, Conn.: Golf Digest/Tennis and Pocket Books.

Watson, T., and Seitz, N. 1992. *Tom Watson's: Getting back to basics*. Trumbull, Conn.: Golf Digest/Tennis, Inc. and Pocket Books Div. of Simon and Schuster.

Wiren, G., and Taylor, D. 1987. *Sure shot: The 100 most common golf mistakes and how to correct them*. Chicago: Contemporary Books.

Wiren, G., and Coop, R. 1979. *The new golf mind*. New York: Simon and Schuster.

# INDEX